Shining Star

B

Assessment Guide

Anna Uhl Chamot

Pam Hartmann

Jann Huizenga

with

Mike Beck

Longman

longman.com

Shining Star ⭐ B

Assessment Guide

Pearson Education, 10 Bank Street, White Plains, NY 10606

Vice president, director of instructional design: Allen Ascher
Editorial director: Ed Lamprich
Acquisitions editor: Amanda Rappaport Dobbins
Project manager: Susan Saslow
Assessment Guide manager: Donna Schaffer
Senior development editors: Susan Clarke Ball, Virginia Bernard
Vice president, director of design and production: Rhea Banker
Executive managing editor: Linda Moser
Production manager: Ray Keating
Senior production editor: Sylvia Dare
Director of manufacturing: Patrice Fraccio
Senior manufacturing buyer: Edith Pullman
Photo research: Kirchoff/Wohlberg, Inc.
Text design and composition: Kirchoff/Wohlberg, Inc.
Cover design: Rhea Banker, Tara Mayer
Text font: 11/14 Franklin Gothic
Illustrations: Liz Callen 7; Robert Casilla 144; Mike DiGiorgio 6; Dorling Kindersley 70, 132; John Hovell 21, 22, 23; Inklink Firenze 14, 148; Mapping Specialists 15; Lyle Miller 146; Craig Spearing 13; Mon-sien Tseng 5.

ISBN: 0-13-184512-8

Printed in the United States of America
2 3 4 5 6 7 8 9 10–BAH–08 07 06 05

CONTENTS

Introduction .... iv–v

Administering the Tests .... v–vi

Listening Passages for Diagnostic Test, Midterm and Final Tests, and Unit Tests .... vii–x

Scoring the Tests xi

Writing Scoring Rubric xii

Building and Assessing Portfolios .... xiii-xiv

Portfolio Assessment Forms .... xv–xvii

My Portfolio (Student Form)

Teacher Portfolio Assessment Form (Teacher Form)

Your Student's Portfolio (Parent or Guardian Form)

Answer Key and Tested Skills Charts .... xviii–xl

Diagnostic Test 3

Midterm Test 11

Final Test 19

Part Tests 27

Unit Tests 77

Test Preparation 139

Taking a Test

Answering Questions About a Passage

Answering Multiple-Choice Items

Answering Questions About Meanings of Words

Answering Fill-in-the-Blank Items

Responding to a Writing Prompt

INTRODUCTION

The *Assessment Guide* provides a variety of tests to help you assess students' understanding of the reading selections and the skills taught in the *Shining Star* program. The Guide was also designed to help students become better test takers. Key test preparation strategies help students become better test takers, by providing them with opportunities to answer questions similar to those found on many standardized tests.

Description of Tests

Diagnostic Test

The Diagnostic Test is based on a readiness for skills taught in Units 1–3. It contains two listening passages: one narrative and one informative. It also includes three reading passages: one narrative, one informative, and one functional. Students answer multiple-choice questions about these passages and about the reading, phonics, spelling, and grammar skills taught in the Student Book. The test ends with a writing prompt based on a type of writing taught in the Student Book. This test provides teachers with a tool for determining which skills individual students or groups of students may need to improve.

Midterm Test

The Midterm Test measures students' proficiency with skills taught in Units 1–3. It contains two listening passages: one narrative and one informative. It also includes three reading passages: one narrative, one informative, and one functional. Students answer multiple-choice questions about these passages and about the reading, phonics, spelling, and grammar skills taught in the Student Book. The test ends with a writing prompt based on a type of writing taught in the Student Book.

Final Test

The Final Test measures students' proficiency with skills taught in Units 4–6. It contains two listening passages: one narrative and one informative. It also includes three reading passages: one narrative, one informative, and one functional. Students answer multiple-choice questions about these passages and about the reading, phonics, spelling, and grammar skills taught in the Student Book. The test ends with a writing prompt based on a type of writing taught in the Student Book.

Part Tests

There are two Part Tests for each unit of the Student Book, twelve Part Tests in all. Each test is based on the skills and reading selections in the first or second part of a unit. Students answer multiple-choice questions about the selections, key vocabulary, reading strategies, genre, literary elements, grammar skills, and writing mechanics presented in the Student Book.

Unit Tests

There is one Unit Test for each unit of the Student Book, six Unit Tests in all. Each test is based on the skills and reading selections from both parts of a unit. It also includes a listening passage, either narrative or informative, that is linked to the unit theme. Students answer multiple-choice questions about the listening passage and the Student Book selections. They also answer questions about phonics skills, spelling skills, key vocabulary, reading strategies, genre, literary elements, and grammar skills. Each test ends with a writing prompt based on a type of writing covered in the unit.

Test Preparation Pages

At the end of this Guide is a section with test preparation strategies. This section raises students' awareness of different kinds of test questions or items and provides them with strategies to use. Sample test questions and a writing prompt are provided, so students can practice applying each strategy.

ADMINISTERING THE TESTS

Planning and Scheduling Tests

Diagnostic Test: Administer the Diagnostic Test at the beginning of the year to assess students' readiness for the skills that will be taught in Units 1–3.

Midterm Test: Administer the Midterm Test after students have finished Unit 3 to assess students' comprehension of the skills taught in Units 1–3 and to measure their progress since taking the Diagnostic Test.

Final Test: Administer the Final Test at the end of the year to assess students' comprehension of the skills taught in Units 4–6 and to measure their progress since taking the Diagnostic Test and the Midterm Test.

Part Tests: Administer each Part Test after finishing the related part in the Student Book.

Unit Tests: Administer each Unit Test after finishing the related unit in the Student Book. The Unit Tests cover the same skills as the Part Tests, but each test has different questions or items. Therefore, you could choose to administer the Unit Test in place of one or both Part Tests or in addition to the two Part Tests. If you are administering the second Part Test, then you should administer the Unit Test after administering the second Part Test.

Test Preparation Pages: The Test Preparation pages can be used at any time during the year prior to taking a test.

The chart below gives an overview of the tests in this *Assessment Guide*. Use the chart to help you plan and schedule the tests. How you choose to administer each test depends on students' needs. For advanced students, you can administer the test as a group and have students read the directions, reading passages, and questions independently. For less proficient students, you may wish to guide them through the test and read aloud the directions, reading passages, and questions as needed. Other options include administering each test in one long session, giving students a short break in the middle, or administering sections of the test in separate sessions over a few days.

Test	Test Sections	Items
Diagnostic Test, Midterm Test, or Final Test	Listening Phonics and Spelling Reading Grammar Writing	2 passages, 8 multiple-choice questions 10 multiple-choice questions 3 passages, 12 multiple-choice questions 8 multiple-choice questions 1 writing prompt
Part Test	Vocabulary Reading Grammar and Writing	6 multiple-choice questions 10 multiple-choice questions 6 multiple-choice questions
Unit Test	Listening Phonics and Spelling Vocabulary Reading Grammar Writing	1 passage, 4 multiple-choice questions 10 multiple-choice questions 8 multiple-choice questions 20 multiple-choice questions 8 multiple-choice questions 1 writing prompt

Directions for Administering the Test

The following directions are general instructions that can be used for all tests. Instructions can be modified, based on how you choose to administer each test.

Before You Administer a Test

Review the test to familiarize yourself with its contents. Make copies of the test for students and yourself. The Diagnostic Test, the Midterm Test, the Final Test, and the Unit Tests each have listening passages that you can read aloud or you can use the program's audio program. If you choose to read a passage aloud, preview it before you administer the test, and have the appropriate passage(s) on hand during the listening section of the test. Listening passages begin on page vii of this Guide. If you use the program's audio program, have the CD and CD-player or the audiocassette and tape-recorder available.

When You Are Ready to Administer a Test

Make sure students' desks are cleared and that they have pens or pencils for marking their tests. The Diagnostic Test, the Midterm Test, the Final Test, and the Unit Tests each have a writing prompt with lines for students' responses. You may wish to provide students with extra lined paper for planning or for additional space to write their responses. Distribute copies of the test to students, and have students write their names on their tests. Describe the contents of the test or the section of the test that you are administering. Point out important features of the test, such as the directions, questions and items, answer choices, writing prompt, and Go On or Stop symbols. Make sure students understand that they are to mark their answers by circling only one letter for each multiple-choice question, and that they should write their response to a writing prompt on the lines below the prompt. Answer any questions that students may have, and then start the test.

If you set a time limit for the test, tell students how much time they have for the test session and write the ending time on the board. Give students a five-minute warning before you end the test session.

After the Test

Directions for scoring the tests are on page xi. Use the Answer Key and Tested Skills Charts that begin on page xviii to score each test. Use the Writing Scoring Rubric on page xii to assess responses to writing prompts in the Diagnostic Test, the Midterm Test, the Final Test, and the Unit Tests.

The Answer Key and Tested Skills Charts can also help you determine students' areas of strength and diagnose problem areas. You may wish to have students add their scored tests to their portfolios. More information about building and assessing portfolios begins on page xiii.

DIRECTIONS

The Diagnostic Test, the Midterm Test, and the Final Test each have two listening passages. Each Unit Test has one listening passage. Read aloud the appropriate listening passage from pages vii–x or have students listen to the recording in the audio program. Read or play each passage twice. After students have listened to the passage twice, pause to allow time for them to answer the items for the passage as you read them aloud. Repeat these steps for the second passage of the Diagnostic Test, the Midterm Test, and the Final Test. After students have finished answering all listening questions, have them continue with the rest of the test.

Diagnostic Test
Passage 1: A Day at the Lake

Tony and his dad went to the lake every year for Tony's birthday. Tony loved going to the lake with his dad. At the lake, they swam in the water and rode in the boat. They ate the lunch that Tony's mom made for them. Sometimes Tony and his dad went fishing. If they caught a big fish, they ate it for dinner. But Tony thought the best part of the day was listening to his dad's stories. Tony's dad told funny stories about things that he did when he was little. Tony laughed at the silly things his dad did. It felt good to spend time with his dad.

Passage 2: Using Lakes for Water, Food, and Fun

Many years ago, huge pieces of ice called glaciers moved slowly over the northern part of Earth. As the glaciers moved, they made large holes, or valleys, in the land. Water filled the valleys to form lakes.

Lakes are very important to plants, animals, and people. Plants grow in lakes. Fish, turtles, insects, and other water animals live in lakes. They eat the plants and, sometimes, they eat each other. Birds and land animals come to the lakes to get drinking water and food. People use water from lakes for drinking, for washing things, and for growing things. They eat fish from lakes. People also have fun on lakes. In the summer, they can ride in boats on lakes or go swimming. In winter, ice forms on the top of some lakes, and people skate on the ice.

Midterm Test
Passage 1: A Trip to the Mountains

Mom and I went on a trip to the mountains. We called it our Mother-Daughter trip. We visited Denver, Colorado. Denver is a city in the Rocky Mountains. Denver is called the Mile-High City because some parts of it are one mile above sea level. Where we live in Ohio, the land is very flat. It was fun to see a place with tall mountains.

We packed sleeping bags, pillows, and lots of warm clothes for the trip. We stayed with Aunt Mary. She has a cabin in the woods near Denver. Aunt Mary drove us high up into the mountains in her car. We skied on snow down part of a mountain. It was scary but exciting to go so fast! We also visited the animals at the Denver Zoo. Before we left, we went to the top of Lookout Mountain Park. From the top of this mountain, people can see the whole city of Denver down below.

Passage 2: The Rocky Mountains

The Rocky Mountains are the largest mountain chain in North America. This chain, or group of mountains, is more than 3,000 miles long. These mountains begin up north in Canada and run south through eight states of the United States and down into Mexico.

The tops of the Rocky Mountains are covered with snow. Mountain goats and bighorn sheep live near the tops of the mountains. Their thick fur keeps them warm, and their strong legs and large hooves help them move up and down rocky paths. Large rivers run down and through the mountains. Green forests and clear, cold lakes lie near the bottom of the mountains. Many animals live in the green forests, such as moose, bears, mountain lions, deer, and elk. Many kinds of fish swim in the rivers and lakes.

Each year many people visit the Rocky Mountains. They come to hunt, fish, ski, climb, or just look at the beautiful mountains.

Final Test

Passage 1: Paul Bunyan and Babe

Do you know how the state of Minnesota got so many lakes? Long ago, a big man named Paul Bunyan and his pet, a big blue ox named Babe, made the lakes. An ox is an animal somewhat like a cow, but stronger.

Paul Bunyan was not just big; he was HUGE. As a child, Paul's shirts were so large that his mother used wagon wheels for buttons. People said that Paul could eat forty bowls of soup—just as a snack! Babe was big, too. All the other farm animals looked like ants when they stood next to Babe.

When Paul grew up, he traveled around the country. He saw many trees. People in Minnesota asked Paul to cut some trees down. They wanted space to build towns. Paul and Babe walked all around Minnesota cutting down trees. Paul and Babe were so big and heavy that when they walked their footsteps made deep holes in the land. Water filled the holes, and the lakes formed. Now Minnesota is called the "Land of 10,000 Lakes."

Passage 2: Trees in North America

In 1607, people crossed the ocean to live in North America. At that time, half of the United States and most of Canada had big forests. Over time, people cut down trees to make space for roads, farms, and towns. They used wood from trees to build things, such as houses, and to burn for heat and cooking.

Today, the United States cuts and uses more wood than any other country. People still use wood to build houses and many other things. Some people still use wood to heat their homes. Paper is made from very tiny pieces of wood, called wood pulp.

But many people worry that we are cutting down too many trees today. Trees in the forests help make the air we breathe. Their roots help keep the soil in place and stop floods. People can help save Earth's trees by supporting laws that protect trees, by using less paper or using recycled paper, and by planting new trees. Trees are important, so let's take care of them.

Unit 1 Test
Passage: The Land Bridge to North America

Thousands of years ago, much of North America was covered with huge sheets of ice. Many large animals lived in North America at that time, but no people lived there. Many areas that are now underwater are thought to have been dry land then. One such area of land now underwater connected North America to Siberia, a region of northern Asia. This area formed a land bridge. Many scientists say that animals used the land bridge, moving back and forth between the two places. Some hunters from Siberia probably started following those animals across the land bridge to North America. Then the climate of Earth became warmer, causing some of the ice sheets to melt. The melting ice caused the water to rise in the Pacific Ocean and cover the land bridge. Over time, some of the people in North America moved south to regions in what is now the United States. Others moved farther south into Central America and South America.

Unit 2 Test
Passage: Making My First Campfire

My family goes camping every year. This year, my brother Carl and I get to make the fire we use to cook our food. Dad tells us how to make a safe campfire.

Dad says, "First, dig a pit, or hole, in the ground so your fire won't spread. Next, place a small pile of twigs and bark in the pit. These small pieces are called tinder, and they catch fire easily. Then, put larger pieces of wood around the tinder. These larger pieces are called kindling. Put the tops of the kindling together in the shape of a tepee. After that, place four big pieces of firewood to make a square around the tepee. Use a match to light the tinder. Once the fire starts, keep adding firewood."

We follow Dad's steps. Carl puts a burning match on the tinder. We see a small flame, and then the wood starts to burn. We did it! We made a fire!

Unit 3 Test
Passage: George Washington Carver, Scientist

George Washington Carver started life as a slave, but he became a famous scientist and inventor. Carver's family worked as slaves on a plantation. His father died when George was a baby, and later his mother was taken away. After slavery ended, Carver went to a school for African American children, and he worked on a farm. Later, Carver studied farming in college. Then he became a teacher and a researcher at a college in Tuskegee, Alabama.

Carver found that cotton crops used up important parts of the soil—the dirt that plants grow in. Growing cotton crops every year harmed the soil. Carver told farmers to grow peanuts and sweet potatoes in some years instead of cotton. Rotating, or changing, the crops made the soil better and helped farmers grow better crops.

Then Carver helped farmers sell their peanuts and sweet potatoes by finding new ways to use these crops. He invented more than 300 new products using peanuts, such as cooking oil, ink, and soap. He discovered more than 100 new ways to use sweet potatoes. Carver died in 1943.

Unit 4 Test
Passage: A New Kind of Transportation

In 2001, people saw a new way for humans to get around. The Segway™ Human Transport looks like a two-wheel scooter, but its tiny computers decide how the driver wants to move. The driver stands on a bar between the two wheels and grabs the handles. When the driver leans forward, the machine goes forward. When the driver leans back, the machine stops. The computers follow the movements of the driver's body. The Segway can travel about twelve miles per hour.

Dean Kamen, the inventor of the Segway, hopes people will use his machine to drive short distances. He thinks the Segway will help cities that have traffic problems. The Segway also helps Earth's environment because its battery stores electricity for energy. If people use the Segway instead of their cars, they will burn less gasoline each year. Earth's air will be cleaner, and we'll save more of Earth's natural resources.

Unit 5 Test
Passage: Jesse's Journal
October 7, 1867

Rusty, our cook, had everyone up at sunrise. After we ate, a thunderstorm started. The loud noise scared the cattle, and they began to stampede. We rushed after the running cattle on our horses. We raced in front of the herd, waving our hats and shooting our guns in the air. This new noise startled the cattle and made them stop. It took a few hours to get the herd back together and moving in the right direction.

At sunset, we made camp. We moved the cattle into a tighter group for the night, and a few cowboys sang to keep the herd calm. Rusty cooked the usual supper—beans, bacon, and biscuits. Now, I'll put my bedroll on the ground next to my horse Lucky and get some sleep.

It will take another month to drive the cattle to Abilene, Kansas. Then, trains will carry the cattle east, and my boss will sell them for good money. I won't get paid much, but I'll have enough to buy a haircut, a bath, a good meal, and a soft bed.

Unit 6 Test
Passage: The Sun and the Stars (A South African Myth)

Long ago, a powerful man lived on Earth. He was so powerful that when he raised his arms, strong rays of light shot out from his body. His light was so bright that it made day on Earth.

But as the man grew older, making light made him tired. He started taking long naps. The people on Earth missed the warm heat from his light. They became cold. Then, one day, a group of children found the man while he was sleeping. They threw him up high into the eastern sky. The man loved being in the sky. Soon he grew strong and bright again. He became the round yellow sun.

Each day, the man traveled west sharing his light with everyone. At the end of each day, he traveled back east high above the sky, and the sky turned dark. But as he moved, his bright light shined through tiny holes in the dark sky and made stars. To this day, the sun rises in the east each morning and sets in the west each night.

SCORING THE TESTS

Use the Answer Key and Tested Skills Charts that begin on page xviii of this Guide and the Writing Scoring Rubric on page xii to help you score students' tests. To score a test, follow these steps:

1. Find the appropriate Answer Key and Tested Skills Chart for the test to be scored. Make a copy of this chart for each student. Write the student's name at the top of the chart.

2. Check the student's answer for each multiple-choice item against the correct answer listed on the chart. Circle the student's score for each multiple-choice item on the chart. Award 1 point for each correct answer and 0 points for any incorrect answers.

3. The Diagnostic Test, the Midterm Test, the Final Test, and the Unit Tests each have a writing prompt in addition to multiple-choice questions. Use the Writing Scoring Rubric on page xii of this Guide to assess the student's response to the prompt. Award the student a score from 0 to 4 points for the response, and circle that score on the chart.

4. Use the formula below the chart to help you calculate a percent score for each test. Add the points circled to find the student's total score for the test and mark that total in the first blank in the formula. Then, divide the total score by the total number of possible points that a student could earn on the test. Finally, multiply the quotient by 100 to get a percent score for the test.

Interpreting Test Results

A student's percent score on a test provides only one measurement of the student's progress and should be interpreted along with other assessments and observations. Students with consistently high scores may need more challenging assignments. Students with consistently low scores probably need a closer review of their progress and perhaps additional instruction and practice.

Use the student's completed Answer Key and Tested Skills Chart as a diagnostic tool. Each test item has been linked to a tested skill. Review the tested skills for the items the student answers correctly as well as for the items answered incorrectly. Look for patterns in the tested skills that indicate the student's strengths, as well as areas where the student may require additional instruction and practice. Use the following resources as needed to provide students with instruction, practice, or support.

- Student Book
- Annotated Teacher's Edition
- Workbook
- Audio Program
- CD-ROM

Note that the Annotated Teacher's Edition provides suggestions for advanced students.

WRITING SCORING RUBRIC

Use the following rubric to help you assess students' responses to the writing prompts in the Diagnostic Test, the Midterm Test, the Final Test, and the Unit Tests. Each response should receive a score from 0 to 4 points, with 4 points being the highest score.

Score	Description
4 points	The composition as a whole is focused, well organized, and complete. Ideas flow in a logical order and use good transitions. The composition includes meaningful choices of words, phrases, and sentences. The student demonstrates a consistent command of spelling, capitalization, punctuation, grammar, usage, and sentence structure. The composition may include some errors in writing conventions, but these errors do not detract from the overall fluency.
3 points	The composition as a whole is focused and complete, but is not as well organized as a 4-point response. Most of the ideas flow logically, but the composition may also include some repetition or have some ideas that are less developed than others. The composition uses appropriate choices for words, phrases, and sentences. The student demonstrates a generally good command of spelling, capitalization, punctuation, grammar, usage, and sentence structure. The composition may include minor errors in writing conventions, but these errors create few disruptions in fluency.
2 points	The composition shows some sense of focus, organization, and completeness. The student may shift suddenly from idea to idea without a logical or smooth transition, but the reader can still understand how the ideas in the composition are related. The composition may also include irrelevant information, repetition, and gaps in ideas, or simply list ideas with little development. The student demonstrates a limited command of writing conventions, and there are errors in spelling, capitalization, punctuation, grammar, usage, and sentence structure throughout the composition. These errors may not cause the writing to be unclear, but they weaken the overall fluency of the composition.
1 point	The composition as a whole is not focused and has little or no sense of completeness or organization. The student may shift suddenly from idea to idea without logical transitions, making it difficult for the reader to understand how the ideas in the composition are related. The student may present ideas in a random or haphazard way or repeat many ideas. The composition may also include many irrelevant ideas or omit relevant information. There is little or no evidence that the student can correctly apply writing conventions. Severe and/or frequent errors in spelling, capitalization, punctuation, grammar, usage, and sentence structure may cause the writing to be unclear or difficult to read. These errors weaken the composition by causing an overall lack of fluency.
0 points	The composition is completely incorrect, irrelevant, or incoherent, or the student does not attempt to respond to the writing prompt at all.

BUILDING AND ASSESSING PORTFOLIOS

How to Use Portfolios

A portfolio is a chronological collection of each student's classroom work and homework throughout the year. You can use portfolios to help you:

- measure students' growth and progress
- determine students' strengths and needs
- customize instructional plans for individual students
- support or elaborate other formal or informal assessments of students
- encourage students to take a more active role in their learning
- provide students with opportunities for self-assessment, making them more aware of their growth and progress and helping them set goals for future improvements
- share a variety of representative examples of students' day-to-day work with parents and explain their child's growth and progress
- share relevant information with teachers that the students will have for the next academic year

What to Include in Portfolios

Portfolios should include a wide variety of students' work in different stages of development, in different media, and for different areas of learning, such as reading, writing, listening, speaking, viewing, and research. Some possible items that students can include in their portfolios are:

- lists of vocabulary words learned with definitions and example sentences
- lists of books read either in class or as independent reading with story summaries and students' personal opinions
- charts, timelines, word webs, and other graphic organizers that record students' ideas about selections they have read or plans for a writing assignment or a workshop activity
- written responses to questions about Student Book selections or work completed for grammar, spelling, and phonics lessons
- writing assignments, including planning information, drafts, revisions and edits, and finished or published work
- drawings or other visuals created for classroom work, homework, presentations, or other activities
- corrected tests or workbook pages
- photographs, audiotapes, and/or videotapes of students reading aloud, discussing ideas in groups, presenting project and workshop activities, responding to presentations by others, or doing other activities
- peer assessments of the student's writing, presentations, group work, or other activities
- self-assessments of the student's strengths, weaknesses, progress, goals, and strategies for achieving goals
- teacher's assessments of the portfolio
- parent's or guardian's comments on the portfolio

How to Manage Students' Portfolios

At the beginning of the year, explain what a portfolio is and how each student will build a portfolio throughout the year. Show students copies of the student, teacher, and parent or guardian portfolio assessment forms on pages xv–xvii of this Guide. Explain that students will choose things that they wish to put in their portfolios throughout the year and that you and their parents will be looking at their portfolios to check their work and progress.

Discuss any previous experiences students may have had building portfolios. Ask them to share what they liked or didn't like about the process. Make sure students understand that their portfolios will show their progress over time. Explain that the items in the portfolio don't have to be finished work, and they don't have to be perfect. Explain that the items in their portfolios should show different stages of the students' work, work that students are proud of, work that shows improvement, and even work that shows areas where the students know they need to work harder. You may wish to pass around portfolio examples that former students have collected in their portfolios, but be sure to obtain permission from these students before sharing any of their work.

Create a set of portfolio folders or boxes that you can keep private when not in use. Establish regular times throughout the year when students will examine their portfolios and add to them. For example, you may wish to have students check and update their portfolios at the end of each part of the unit or at the end of each unit. Be sure you give students an opportunity to update their portfolios just before the end of a grading period or before a student or parent conference. Have students complete a copy of the student portfolio assessment form on page xv for each item they wish to include in their portfolios and attach this form to their items.

Establish regular times when you will assess the contents of students' portfolios. Review the work in the portfolio and assess students' growth and progress since your last review. Use the teacher portfolio assessment form on page xvi of this Guide to help you assess students' focus, portfolio variety, attitude, and progress, and to award each portfolio an overall score from 1 to 4 points.

Establish regular times when students will select parts of their portfolio to take home and share with their family. Give suggestions about some items to take home, so parents are able to see a good variety of students' work. Make copies of the parent portfolio assessment form on page xvii of this Guide and include your own comments about the students' portfolios, giving examples of items that demonstrate students' strengths and progress and identifying areas that need further work. Give students the parent form and have them return this form with their parents' or guardians' signatures. You may wish to make an inventory of the items that students are removing from their portfolios, so you can make sure that all items are properly returned after the home review. You can also share portfolios with parents during conferences.

At the end of the year, give students an opportunity to review their completed portfolios. Help them choose some items that you will share with the teachers they will have next year and other items that they will take home. You may also wish to select a few items that students will allow you to share with the students you will have the next year. The remaining items can be discarded. Discuss with students what they learned from building a portfolio and their goals for the next year.

Name _____ Date _____

MY PORTFOLIO

DIRECTIONS

Choose an item for your portfolio. The item should be something that shows your work for the class. It doesn't have to be perfect. It just needs to have one thing that you are proud of. Your portfolio will show your progress over the year. Include different stages of your work so you can show how you made your work better or show how much you have learned. Use this form to tell about the item, your work for the class, and your portfolio. Then attach this form to your item and put it in your portfolio.

1. The item I chose for my portfolio is _____
    _____.

2. I chose this item because _____
    _____.

3. I am proud of this work because _____
    _____.

4. Some things I learned from doing this work are _____
    _____.

5. Some things that others told me about my work are _____
    _____.

6. One way my work has changed is that _____
    _____.

7. Some things that I do well are _____
    _____.

8. Some things that I need to improve are _____
    _____.

9. My goals for the future are _____
    _____.

10. The most important thing that I learned from building a portfolio is _____
    _____.

Student's Name _____

Teacher's Name _____

TEACHER PORTFOLIO ASSESSMENT FORM

DIRECTIONS

Assess each student's portfolio on a regular basis. Note the date of each assessment in the chart. Use the rubrics below the chart to help you determine a score of 1 to 4 points for focus, variety, attitude, and progress. Then use these scores to determine an overall score for the portfolio. Circle each score in the chart. Add comments about the best work in the portfolio, areas that need improvement, and any other observations. Share the results of your assessment with students and parents during student or parent conferences.

Date	Focus	Variety	Attitude	Progress	Overall Score	Comments
	1 2 3 4	1 2 3 4	1 2 3 4	1 2 3 4	1 2 3 4	
	1 2 3 4	1 2 3 4	1 2 3 4	1 2 3 4	1 2 3 4	
	1 2 3 4	1 2 3 4	1 2 3 4	1 2 3 4	1 2 3 4	
	1 2 3 4	1 2 3 4	1 2 3 4	1 2 3 4	1 2 3 4	
	1 2 3 4	1 2 3 4	1 2 3 4	1 2 3 4	1 2 3 4	
	1 2 3 4	1 2 3 4	1 2 3 4	1 2 3 4	1 2 3 4	

Focus	Variety	Attitude	Progress
4 Items reflect a clear set of goals and a focused strategy for attaining them.	**4** Items are highly varied and demonstrate competence and creativity in many areas.	**4** Student shows enthusiasm and commitment to achieving stated goals.	**4** Shows substantial progress over previous work in a broad range of skills and competencies.
3 Most items reflect the stated goals, but also include some unproductive strategies.	**3** Items reflect some variety and demonstrate competence and creativity in several areas.	**3** Student shows a generally positive attitude about achieving goals, but shows occasional periods of inactivity or low interest.	**3** Shows measurable growth and progress in several areas of skills and competencies.
2 Goals lack clarity and strategies have regular lapses in focus.	**2** Items are generally of one type with some new competencies and/or occasional creativity.	**2** Student needs regular urging or reminders to complete portfolio forms and add items to portfolios.	**2** Modest growth or progress in one or two areas.
1 No consistent goal and generally aimless activities in portfolio.	**1** Items are of one type and show little or no concern for creativity.	**1** Student is completely lacking in enthusiasm and commitment; only works on portfolio after repeated reminders.	**1** No noticeable growth in any area; work is mechanical and repetitive.

YOUR STUDENT'S PORTFOLIO

Dear Parent or Guardian,

Your student is making a portfolio. This portfolio includes examples of your student's work at different stages throughout the year. The student chooses items that he or she wants in the portfolio and includes an explanation about why these items were chosen. Each student also includes his or her thoughts about the things he or she does well and areas that may need more work. I will be using this portfolio to check your student's growth and progress during the school year.

Here are a few items from your student's portfolio with my comments about his or her work and progress. Review these items with him or her and discuss my comments. Ask what he or she likes about each item included and decide on some goals for making the work better. After you have finished discussing this work, sign your name at the bottom of this letter. Please add any comments or suggestions you have about the portfolio or my comments. Then have your student return the signed letter and the portfolio items to me.

The student's portfolio is an important part of his or her class work this year. Thank you for discussing it with him or her.

Sincerely,

_____

Teacher

COMMENTS FROM THE TEACHER
Items From Your Student's Portfolio

_____

_____

How These Items Show the Student's Strength and Progress

_____

_____

Areas Where the Student Needs More Work

_____

_____

COMMENTS FROM THE PARENT OR GUARDIAN

I discussed these items and your comments with my student. Here are some of my thoughts:

_____

_____

Parent's or Guardian's Signature _____

Parent or Guardian Portfolio Assessment Form

Student's Name _____

DIAGNOSTIC TEST Answer Key and Tested Skills Chart

ITEM	ANSWER	TESTED SKILL	SCORE (Circle one.)
Listening			
1.	C	Setting	0 1
2.	D	Supporting Details	0 1
3.	A	Characterization	0 1
4.	A	Making Inferences	0 1
5.	C	Context Clues	0 1
6.	A	Sequence	0 1
7.	B	Cause and Effect	0 1
8.	C	Main Idea	0 1
Phonics			
9.	C	Short *a*	0 1
10.	B	Short *o*	0 1
11.	A	Silent *e*	0 1
12.	D	*r*-controlled Vowels	0 1
13.	A	Digraph *wh*	0 1
Spelling			
14.	C	Long and Short *a, e*	0 1
15.	D	Long and Short *i*	0 1
16.	B	Long and Short *o, u*	0 1
17.	C	Adding *-ed*	0 1
18.	A	Initial *w, j*	0 1
Reading			
19.	B	Visualizing	0 1
20.	A	Making Inferences	0 1
21.	C	Flashbacks	0 1
22.	D	Predicting	0 1
23.	B	Context Clues	0 1
24.	A	Previewing	0 1
25.	A	Making Inferences	0 1
26.	A	Skimming	0 1
27.	A	Understanding a Poster	0 1
28.	B	Understanding a Poster	0 1
29.	B	Context Clues	0 1
30.	A	Monitoring Your Comprehension	0 1
Grammar			
31.	A	Pronouns	0 1
32.	B	Pronouns	0 1
33.	C	Conjunction *and*	0 1
34.	B	Subject-Verb Agreement: Simple Present	0 1
35.	C	Sequence Words	0 1
36.	D	*Wh-* Questions: Simple Past	0 1
37.	A	Conjunction *or*	0 1
38.	B	Compound Sentences	0 1
Writing	See p. xii.	Descriptive Writing	0 1 2 3 4

_____ ÷ **42** X **100** = _____
(Student's Total Score)   (Total Possible Points)   (Student's Percent Score)

Student's Name _____

MIDTERM TEST Answer Key and Tested Skills Chart

ITEM	ANSWER	TESTED SKILL	SCORE (Circle one.)
Listening			
1.	D	Supporting Details	0 1
2.	C	Supporting Details	0 1
3.	D	Making Inferences	0 1
4.	B	Point of View	0 1
5.	B	Context Clues	0 1
6.	A	Supporting Details	0 1
7.	C	Genre	0 1
8.	C	Making Inferences	0 1
Phonics			
9.	D	Long *i*	0 1
10.	C	Short *o*	0 1
11.	A	Silent *e*	0 1
12.	B	*r*-controlled Vowels	0 1
13.	C	Digraph *wh*	0 1
Spelling			
14.	D	Long and Short *a, e*	0 1
15.	C	Long and Short *i*	0 1
16.	D	Long and Short *o, u*	0 1
17.	B	Adding *-ed*	0 1
18.	A	Occupation Words	0 1
Reading			
19.	B	Main Idea	0 1
20.	D	Visualizing	0 1
21.	B	Predicting	0 1
22.	C	Identifying with a Character	0 1
23.	D	Supporting Details	0 1
24.	A	Genre	0 1
25.	B	Making Inferences	0 1
26.	C	Skimming	0 1
27.	A	Interpreting a Map	0 1
28.	C	Interpreting a Map	0 1
29.	D	Interpreting a Map	0 1
30.	D	Interpreting a Map	0 1
Grammar			
31.	B	Pronouns	0 1
32.	C	Pronouns	0 1
33.	A	Conjunction *and*	0 1
34.	B	Subject-Verb Agreement: Simple Present	0 1
35.	D	Sequence Words	0 1
36.	A	*Wh-* Questions: Simple Past	0 1
37.	B	Compound Sentences	0 1
38.	D	Compound Sentences	0 1
Writing	See p. xii.	Narrative Writing	0 1 2 3 4

_____ ÷ **42** X **100** = _____
(Student's Total Score)   (Total Possible Points)   (Student's Percent Score)

Midterm Test/Answer Key and Tested Skills Chart

Student's Name _____

FINAL TEST Answer Key and Tested Skills Chart

ITEM	ANSWER	TESTED SKILL	SCORE (Circle one.)
Listening			
1.	A	Compare and Contrast	0 1
2.	C	Cause and Effect	0 1
3.	D	Plot	0 1
4.	D	Genre	0 1
5.	D	Cause and Effect	0 1
6.	A	Supporting Details	0 1
7.	C	Cause and Effect	0 1
8.	C	Main Idea	0 1
Phonics			
9.	C	Schwa	0 1
10.	A	Voiced and Unvoiced Final *s*	0 1
11.	C	Blends	0 1
12.	D	Digraphs *ch, tch*	0 1
13.	B	Diphthongs *oo, ou, ow, oy, oi*	0 1
Spelling			
14.	A	Schwa	0 1
15.	D	Plurals	0 1
16.	B	Adding *-er* and *-est*	0 1
17.	C	*kn-* Words	0 1
18.	D	Adding *-ing*	0 1
Reading			
19.	B	Making Inferences	0 1
20.	B	Simile	0 1
21.	B	Supporting Details	0 1
22.	C	Using Your Experience to Understand a Story	0 1
23.	B	Genre	0 1
24.	A	Chronology	0 1
25.	D	Context Clues	0 1
26.	B	Summarizing	0 1
27.	B	Studying Diagrams	0 1
28.	B	Studying Diagrams	0 1
29.	B	Studying Diagrams	0 1
30.	D	Studying Diagrams	0 1
Grammar			
31.	C	Real Conditionals	0 1
32.	B	Comparative Adjectives	0 1
33.	B	Prepositional Phrases	0 1
34.	A	Possessive Pronouns	0 1
35.	D	Possessive Adjectives	0 1
36.	C	Complex Sentences	0 1
37.	A	Superlative Adjectives	0 1
38.	B	Quotations	0 1
Writing	See p. xii.	Writing to Entertain	0 1 2 3 4

_____ ÷ **42** X **100** = _____

(Student's Total Score)   (Total Possible Points)   (Student's Percent Score)

Student's Name _____

UNIT 1 PART 1 TEST Answer Key and Tested Skills Chart

ITEM	ANSWER	TESTED SKILL	SCORE (Circle one.)
Vocabulary			
1.	C	Classifying	0 1
2.	B	Classifying	0 1
3.	D	Context Clues	0 1
4.	B	Context Clues	0 1
5.	A	Context Clues	0 1
6.	C	Context Clues	0 1
Reading			
7.	D	Genre	0 1
8.	A	Supporting Details	0 1
9.	C	Cause and Effect	0 1
10.	D	Cause and Effect	0 1
11.	B	Author's Purpose	0 1
12.	C	Previewing and Predicting	0 1
13.	A	Genre	0 1
14.	B	Alliteration	0 1
15.	D	Main Idea	0 1
16.	C	Making Inferences	0 1
Grammar			
17.	D	Pronouns	0 1
18.	A	Pronouns	0 1
19.	D	Pronouns	0 1
20.	B	Pronouns	0 1
Writing			
21.	A	Capitalization and End Marks	0 1
22.	C	Adjective Placement and Form	0 1

_____ ÷ **22** X **100** = _____
(Student's Total Score)   (Total Possible Points)   (Student's Percent Score)

Student's Name _____

UNIT 1 PART 2 TEST Answer Key and Tested Skills Chart

ITEM	ANSWER	TESTED SKILL	SCORE (Circle one.)
Vocabulary			
1.	D	Classifying	0 1
2.	B	Classifying	0 1
3.	C	Context Clues	0 1
4.	B	Context Clues	0 1
5.	D	Context Clues	0 1
6.	A	Context Clues	0 1
Reading			
7.	D	Supporting Details	0 1
8.	B	Cause and Effect	0 1
9.	D	Visualizing	0 1
10.	B	Flashbacks	0 1
11.	C	Making Inferences	0 1
12.	C	Genre	0 1
13.	B	Main Idea	0 1
14.	C	Supporting Details	0 1
15.	A	Supporting Details	0 1
16.	D	Understanding a Map	0 1
Grammar			
17.	D	Conjunction *and*	0 1
18.	B	Conjunction *or*	0 1
19.	C	Conjunction *and*	0 1
20.	A	Conjunction *or*	0 1
Writing			
21.	B	End Marks	0 1
22.	D	Capitalization	0 1

_____ ÷ **22** X **100** = _____
(Student's Total Score)   (Total Possible Points)   (Student's Percent Score)

UNIT 2 PART 1 TEST Answer Key and Tested Skills Chart

ITEM	ANSWER	TESTED SKILL	SCORE (Circle one.)
Vocabulary			
1.	A	Classifying	0 1
2.	C	Classifying	0 1
3.	B	Greek/Latin Roots	0 1
4.	A	Greek/Latin Roots	0 1
5.	D	Greek/Latin Roots	0 1
6.	B	Greek/Latin Roots	0 1
Reading			
7.	D	Genre	0 1
8.	C	Compare and Contrast	0 1
9.	B	Supporting Details	0 1
10.	D	Making Inferences	0 1
11.	A	Supporting Details	0 1
12.	C	Skimming	0 1
13.	B	Rhyme	0 1
14.	D	Supporting Details	0 1
15.	B	Literary Element	0 1
16.	C	Making Inferences	0 1
Grammar			
17.	A	Subject-Verb Agreement: Simple Present	0 1
18.	A	Subject-Verb Agreement: Simple Present	0 1
19.	C	Subject-Verb Agreement: Simple Present	0 1
20.	B	Subject-Verb Agreement: Simple Present	0 1
Writing			
21.	D	Capitalization	0 1
22.	B	Capitalization	0 1

_____   ÷   **22**   X   **100**   =   _____
(Student's Total Score)   (Total Possible Points)   (Student's Percent Score)

UNIT 2 PART 2 TEST Answer Key and Tested Skills Chart

ITEM	ANSWER	TESTED SKILL	SCORE (Circle one.)
Vocabulary			
1.	B	Classifying	0 1
2.	A	Classifying	0 1
3.	D	Context Clues	0 1
4.	A	Context Clues	0 1
5.	C	Context Clues	0 1
6.	D	Context Clues	0 1
Reading			
7.	D	Plot	0 1
8.	A	Plot	0 1
9.	B	Plot	0 1
10.	D	Personification	0 1
11.	C	Characterization	0 1
12.	D	Identifying with a Character	0 1
13.	C	Supporting Details	0 1
14.	B	Main Idea	0 1
15.	A	Summarizing	0 1
16.	D	Genre	0 1
Grammar			
17.	C	Adverbs	0 1
18.	B	Adverbs	0 1
19.	A	Adverbs	0 1
20.	D	Adverbs	0 1
Writing			
21.	B	Frequency Adverbs	0 1
22.	A	Frequency Adverbs	0 1

_____   ÷   **22**   X   **100**   =   _____

(Student's Total Score)　　　(Total Possible Points)　　　　　(Student's Percent Score)

UNIT 3 PART 1 TEST Answer Key and Tested Skills Chart

ITEM	ANSWER	TESTED SKILL	SCORE (Circle one.)
Vocabulary			
1.	C	Classifying	0 1
2.	D	Classifying	0 1
3.	C	Context Clues	0 1
4.	C	Context Clues	0 1
5.	A	Context Clues	0 1
6.	D	Context Clues	0 1
Reading			
7.	C	Genre	0 1
8.	B	Supporting Details	0 1
9.	A	Making Inferences	0 1
10.	D	Making Inferences	0 1
11.	D	Making Inferences	0 1
12.	C	Cause and Effect	0 1
13.	D	Genre	0 1
14.	A	Supporting Details	0 1
15.	B	Making Inferences	0 1
16.	C	Summarizing	0 1
Grammar			
17.	C	*Wh-* Questions in the Simple Past	0 1
18.	B	*Wh-* Questions in the Simple Past	0 1
19.	A	*Wh-* Questions in the Simple Past	0 1
20.	D	*Yes/No* Questions in the Simple Past	0 1
Writing			
21.	D	End Punctuation	0 1
22.	C	Questions	0 1

_____ ÷ **22** X **100** = _____

(Student's Total Score) (Total Possible Points) (Student's Percent Score)

UNIT 3 PART 2 TEST Answer Key and Tested Skills Chart

ITEM	ANSWER	TESTED SKILL	SCORE (Circle one.)
Vocabulary			
1.	A	Classifying	0 1
2.	C	Classifying	0 1
3.	D	Context Clues	0 1
4.	A	Context Clues	0 1
5.	B	Context Clues	0 1
6.	C	Context Clues	0 1
Reading			
7.	C	Genre	0 1
8.	A	Point of View	0 1
9.	D	Main Idea	0 1
10.	A	Summarizing	0 1
11.	B	Cause and Effect	0 1
12.	D	Monitoring Comprehension	0 1
13.	D	Supporting Details	0 1
14.	D	Supporting Details	0 1
15.	B	Steps in a Process	0 1
16.	C	Steps in a Process	0 1
Grammar			
17.	C	Compound Sentences	0 1
18.	A	Compound Sentences	0 1
19.	B	Compound Sentences	0 1
20.	D	Compound Sentences	0 1
Writing			
21.	B	Commas in Compound Sentences	0 1
22.	C	Commas in Compound Sentences	0 1

_____ ÷ **22** X **100** = _____

(Student's Total Score) (Total Possible Points) (Student's Percent Score)

Student's Name _____

UNIT 4 PART 1 TEST Answer Key and Tested Skills Chart

ITEM	ANSWER	TESTED SKILL	SCORE (Circle one.)
Vocabulary			
1.	D	Classifying	0 1
2.	C	Classifying	0 1
3.	D	Context Clues	0 1
4.	B	Context Clues	0 1
5.	A	Context Clues	0 1
6.	C	Context Clues	0 1
Reading			
7.	D	Genre	0 1
8.	A	Summarizing	0 1
9.	C	Cause and Effect	0 1
10.	A	Cause and Effect	0 1
11.	C	Compare and Contrast	0 1
12.	B	Supporting Details	0 1
13.	B	Summarizing	0 1
14.	A	Cause and Effect	0 1
15.	C	Compare and Contrast	0 1
16.	D	Author's Purpose	0 1
Grammar			
17.	C	Real Conditionals	0 1
18.	A	Real Conditionals	0 1
19.	C	Real Conditionals	0 1
20.	B	Real Conditionals	0 1
Writing			
21.	A	Commas in Real Conditionals	0 1
22.	D	Commas in Real Conditionals	0 1

_____ ÷ **22** X **100** = _____
(Student's Total Score)   (Total Possible Points)   (Student's Percent Score)

Student's Name _____

UNIT 4 PART 2 TEST Answer Key and Tested Skills Chart

ITEM	ANSWER	TESTED SKILL	SCORE (Circle one.)
Vocabulary			
1.	D	Classifying	0 1
2.	C	Classifying	0 1
3.	D	Context Clues	0 1
4.	A	Context Clues	0 1
5.	B	Context Clues	0 1
6.	A	Context Clues	0 1
Reading			
7.	B	Genre	0 1
8.	D	Main Idea	0 1
9.	D	Making Inferences	0 1
10.	C	Dialogue	0 1
11.	C	Simile	0 1
12.	A	Using Your Experience to Understand a Story	0 1
13.	D	Summarizing	0 1
14.	A	Generalizing	0 1
15.	D	Supporting Details	0 1
16.	A	Supporting Details	0 1
Grammar			
17.	A	Complex Sentences	0 1
18.	D	Complex Sentences	0 1
19.	C	Complex Sentences	0 1
20.	B	Complex Sentences	0 1
Writing			
21.	C	Commas in Complex Sentences	0 1
22.	A	Commas in Complex Sentences	0 1

_____ ÷ **22** X **100** = _____
(Student's Total Score)   (Total Possible Points)   (Student's Percent Score)

Student's Name _____

UNIT 5 PART 1 TEST Answer Key and Tested Skills Chart

ITEM	ANSWER	TESTED SKILL	SCORE (Circle one.)
Vocabulary			
1.	C	Classifying	0 1
2.	A	Classifying	0 1
3.	B	Context Clues	0 1
4.	C	Context Clues	0 1
5.	D	Context Clues	0 1
6.	D	Context Clues	0 1
Reading			
7.	D	Genre	0 1
8.	A	Cause and Effect	0 1
9.	B	Cause and Effect	0 1
10.	C	Summarizing	0 1
11.	B	Supporting Details	0 1
12.	C	Taking Notes	0 1
13.	C	Genre	0 1
14.	B	Setting	0 1
15.	B	Supporting Details	0 1
16.	D	Making Inferences	0 1
Grammar			
17.	B	Comparative Adjectives	0 1
18.	A	Superlative Adjectives	0 1
19.	C	Comparative Adjectives	0 1
20.	B	Superlative Adjectives	0 1
Writing			
21.	D	Capitalizing Proper Nouns	0 1
22.	C	Capitalizing Proper Nouns	0 1

_____ ÷ **22** X **100** = _____
(Student's Total Score) (Total Possible Points)   (Student's Percent Score)

UNIT 5 PART 2 TEST Answer Key and Tested Skills Chart

ITEM	ANSWER	TESTED SKILL	SCORE (Circle one.)
Vocabulary			
1.	A	Classifying	0 1
2.	D	Classifying	0 1
3.	C	Context Clues	0 1
4.	B	Context Clues	0 1
5.	D	Context Clues	0 1
6.	C	Context Clues	0 1
Reading			
7.	A	Genre	0 1
8.	C	Sequence of Events	0 1
9.	B	Making Inferences	0 1
10.	B	Summarizing	0 1
11.	C	Character	0 1
12.	D	Hyperbole	0 1
13.	D	Genre	0 1
14.	C	Cause and Effect	0 1
15.	B	Supporting Details	0 1
16.	C	Cause and Effect	0 1
Grammar			
17.	A	Possessive Adjectives	0 1
18.	A	Possessive Adjectives	0 1
19.	C	Possessive Pronouns	0 1
20.	D	Possessive Pronouns	0 1
Writing			
21.	A	Possessive Adjective *its*	0 1
22.	C	Adjective Placement	0 1

_____ ÷ **22** X **100** = _____

(Student's Total Score) (Total Possible Points) (Student's Percent Score)

Student's Name _____

UNIT 6 PART 1 TEST Answer Key and Tested Skills Chart

ITEM	ANSWER	TESTED SKILL	SCORE (Circle one.)
Vocabulary			
1.	D	Classifying	0 1
2.	A	Classifying	0 1
3.	A	Context Clues	0 1
4.	D	Context Clues	0 1
5.	B	Context Clues	0 1
6.	C	Context Clues	0 1
Reading			
7.	B	Genre	0 1
8.	D	Cause and Effect	0 1
9.	C	Supporting Details	0 1
10.	B	Studying Diagrams	0 1
11.	C	Cause and Effect	0 1
12.	A	Supporting Details	0 1
13.	A	Plot	0 1
14.	B	Hero or Heroine	0 1
15.	B	Conflict	0 1
16.	D	Compare and Contrast	0 1
Grammar			
17.	D	Quotations	0 1
18.	C	Quotations	0 1
19.	A	Quotations	0 1
20.	B	Quotations	0 1
Writing			
21.	A	Dialogue	0 1
22.	B	Dialogue	0 1

_____ ÷ **22** X **100** = _____
(Student's Total Score)   (Total Possible Points)   (Student's Percent Score)

Student's Name _____

ITEM	ANSWER	TESTED SKILL	SCORE (Circle one.)
Vocabulary			
1.	C	Classifying	0 1
2.	B	Classifying	0 1
3.	D	Context Clues	0 1
4.	D	Context Clues	0 1
5.	B	Context Clues	0 1
6.	A	Context Clues	0 1
Reading			
7.	B	Narrator	0 1
8.	C	Stage Directions	0 1
9.	D	Main Idea	0 1
10.	C	Compare and Contrast	0 1
11.	A	Plot	0 1
12.	B	Reading Plays Aloud	0 1
13.	D	Summarizing	0 1
14.	B	Supporting Details	0 1
15.	A	Supporting Details	0 1
16.	A	Cause and Effect	0 1
Grammar			
17.	D	Prepositional Phrases	0 1
18.	B	Prepositional Phrases	0 1
19.	C	Prepositional Phrases	0 1
20.	A	Prepositional Phrases	0 1
Writing			
21.	C	Dialogue	0 1
22.	C	Stage Directions	0 1

_____ ÷ **22** X **100** = _____
(Student's Total Score)   (Total Possible Points)   (Student's Percent Score)

Student's Name _____

UNIT 1 TEST Answer Key and Tested Skills Chart

ITEM	ANSWER	TESTED SKILL	SCORE (Circle one.)
Listening			
1.	A	Supporting Details	0 1
2.	B	Cause and Effect	0 1
3.	C	Cause and Effect	0 1
4.	B	Supporting Details	0 1
Phonics			
5.	B	Long *a*	0 1
6.	D	Long *e*	0 1
7.	A	Short *i*	0 1
8.	C	Long *i*	0 1
9.	D	Short *e*	0 1
Spelling			
10.	A	Short *a*	0 1
11.	D	Long *e*	0 1
12.	B	Long *a*	0 1
13.	C	Long *i*	0 1
14.	A	Short *i*	0 1
Vocabulary			
15.	C	Word Meaning	0 1
16.	B	Word Meaning	0 1
17.	D	Word Meaning	0 1
18.	A	Word Meaning	0 1
19.	C	Context Clues	0 1
20.	B	Context Clues	0 1
21.	D	Context Clues	0 1
22.	C	Context Clues	0 1
Reading			
23.	C	Supporting Details	0 1
24.	D	Supporting Details	0 1
25.	A	Making Inferences	0 1
26.	D	Supporting Details	0 1
27.	B	Previewing and Predicting	0 1
28.	B	Genre	0 1
29.	C	Summarizing	0 1
30.	D	Alliteration	0 1
31.	B	Making Inferences	0 1
32.	C	Author's Viewpoint	0 1
33.	D	Genre	0 1
34.	A	Plot	0 1
35.	D	Flashbacks	0 1
36.	C	Visualizing	0 1
37.	A	Making Inferences	0 1
38.	B	Main Idea	0 1
39.	D	Genre	0 1
40.	D	Main Idea	0 1
41.	B	Understanding a Map	0 1
42.	C	Making Inferences	0 1
Grammar			
43.	A	Pronouns	0 1
44.	D	Pronouns	0 1
45.	B	Pronouns	0 1
46.	B	Conjunction *and*	0 1
47.	A	Conjunction *or*	0 1
48.	C	Pronouns	0 1
49.	A	Conjunction *or*	0 1
50.	D	Conjunction *and*	0 1
Writing	See p. xii.	Descriptive Writing	0 1 2 3 4

_____ ÷ **54** X **100** = _____
(Student's Total Score)　(Total Possible Points)　　　(Student's Percent Score)

Student's Name _____

UNIT 2 TEST Answer Key and Tested Skills Chart

ITEM	ANSWER	TESTED SKILL	SCORE (Circle one.)
Listening			
1.	B	Supporting Details	0 1
2.	A	Steps in a Process	0 1
3.	B	Steps in a Process	0 1
4.	D	Making Inferences	0 1
Phonics			
5.	B	Short *o*	0 1
6.	C	Long *o*	0 1
7.	A	Short *u*	0 1
8.	D	Long *u*	0 1
9.	D	Silent *e*	0 1
Spelling			
10.	B	Short *u*	0 1
11.	A	Short *o*	0 1
12.	C	Long *u*	0 1
13.	B	Adding -*ed*	0 1
14.	A	Adding -*ed*	0 1
Vocabulary			
15.	C	Greek/Latin Roots	0 1
16.	B	Word Meaning	0 1
17.	D	Word Meaning	0 1
18.	C	Greek/Latin Roots	0 1
19.	C	Context Clues	0 1
20.	D	Context Clues	0 1
21.	A	Context Clues	0 1
22.	A	Context Clues	0 1
Reading			
23.	B	Supporting Details	0 1
24.	D	Compare and Contrast	0 1
25.	C	Supporting Details	0 1
26.	A	Supporting Details	0 1
27.	A	Skimming	0 1
28.	C	Genre	0 1
29.	D	Visualizing	0 1
30.	A	Rhyme	0 1
31.	B	Genre	0 1
32.	A	Visualizing	0 1
33.	A	Setting	0 1
34.	C	Sequence	0 1
35.	B	Plot	0 1
36.	D	Personification	0 1
37.	A	Characterization	0 1
38.	D	Identifying with a Character	0 1
39.	A	Supporting Details	0 1
40.	D	Main Idea	0 1
41.	C	Cause and Effect	0 1
42.	D	Steps in a Process	0 1
Grammar			
43.	B	Subject-Verb Agreement: Present Tense	0 1
44.	A	Subject-Verb Agreement: Present Tense	0 1
45.	C	Adverbs	0 1
46.	B	Adverbs	0 1
47.	B	Adverbs	0 1
48.	B	Subject-Verb Agreement: Present Tense	0 1
49.	A	Subject-Verb Agreement: Present Tense	0 1
50.	B	Adverbs	0 1
Writing	See p. xii.	Expository/How-to Writing	0 1 2 3 4

_____ ÷ **54** X **100** = _____
(Student's Total Score) (Total Possible Points)   (Student's Percent Score)

Student's Name _____

UNIT 3 TEST Answer Key and Tested Skills Chart

ITEM	ANSWER	TESTED SKILL	SCORE (Circle one.)
Listening			
1.	B	Genre	0 1
2.	A	Cause and Effect	0 1
3.	A	Summarizing	0 1
4.	C	Main Idea	0 1
Phonics			
5.	A	*r*-controlled Vowels	0 1
6.	D	*r*-controlled Vowels	0 1
7.	B	*r*-controlled Vowels	0 1
8.	C	Digraph *wh*	0 1
9.	A	Digraph *wh*	0 1
Spelling			
10.	C	Occupation Words	0 1
11.	B	Occupation Words	0 1
12.	B	Occupation Words	0 1
13.	A	Initial *w*	0 1
14.	C	Initial *j*	0 1
Vocabulary			
15.	C	Word Meaning	0 1
16.	A	Word Meaning	0 1
17.	D	Word Meaning	0 1
18.	C	Word Meaning	0 1
19.	D	Context Clues	0 1
20.	B	Context Clues	0 1
21.	B	Context Clues	0 1
22.	A	Context Clues	0 1
Reading			
23.	B	Genre	0 1
24.	A	Supporting Details	0 1
25.	D	Making Inferences	0 1
26.	D	Supporting Details	0 1
27.	A	Supporting Details	0 1
28.	C	Compare and Contrast	0 1
29.	B	Context Clues	0 1
30.	A	Analyzing Text Structure	0 1
31.	A	Supporting Details	0 1
32.	C	Context Clues	0 1
33.	D	Setting	0 1
34.	D	Making Inferences	0 1
35.	C	Plot	0 1
36.	A	Making Inferences	0 1
37.	B	Point of View	0 1
38.	B	Monitoring Your Comprehension	0 1
39.	A	Fact and Opinion	0 1
40.	D	Supporting Details	0 1
41.	C	Steps in a Process	0 1
42.	A	Steps in a Process	0 1
Grammar			
43.	C	*Yes/No* Questions: Simple Past	0 1
44.	A	*Wh-* Questions: Simple Past	0 1
45.	B	*Wh-* Questions: Simple Past	0 1
46.	A	Compound Sentences	0 1
47.	D	Compound Sentences	0 1
48.	C	*Wh-* Questions: Simple Past	0 1
49.	C	Compound Sentences	0 1
50.	C	Compound Sentences	0 1
Writing	See p. xii.	Narrative Writing	0 1 2 3 4

_____ ÷ **54** X **100** = _____

(Student's Total Score)   (Total Possible Points)   (Student's Percent Score)

Student's Name _____

UNIT 4 TEST Answer Key and Tested Skills Chart

ITEM	ANSWER	TESTED SKILL	SCORE (Circle one.)
Listening			
1.	C	Supporting Details	0 1
2.	C	Making Inferences	0 1
3.	B	Supporting Details	0 1
4.	D	Cause and Effect	0 1
Phonics			
5.	B	Schwa	0 1
6.	C	Schwa	0 1
7.	C	Schwa	0 1
8.	D	Voiced and Unvoiced Final s	0 1
9.	B	Voiced and Unvoiced Final s	0 1
Spelling			
10.	A	Schwa	0 1
11.	B	Schwa	0 1
12.	A	Plurals	0 1
13.	C	Plurals	0 1
14.	D	Plurals	0 1
Vocabulary			
15.	B	Word Meaning	0 1
16.	C	Word Meaning	0 1
17.	D	Word Meaning	0 1
18.	A	Word Meaning	0 1
19.	D	Context Clues	0 1
20.	A	Context Clues	0 1
21.	B	Context Clues	0 1
22.	C	Context Clues	0 1
Reading			
23.	B	Genre	0 1
24.	D	Cause and Effect	0 1
25.	A	Cause and Effect	0 1
26.	B	Cause and Effect	0 1
27.	A	Supporting Details	0 1
28.	C	Compare and Contrast	0 1
29.	B	Context Clues	0 1
30.	A	Making Inferences	0 1
31.	D	Supporting Details	0 1
32.	A	Author's Purpose	0 1
33.	D	Making Inferences	0 1
34.	B	Dialogue	0 1
35.	C	Simile	0 1
36.	B	Plot	0 1
37.	C	Plot	0 1
38.	D	Using Your Experience to Understand a Story	0 1
39.	D	Genre	0 1
40.	A	Supporting Details	0 1
41.	B	Summarizing	0 1
42.	A	Understanding a Bar Graph	0 1
Grammar			
43.	C	Real Conditionals	0 1
44.	A	Real Conditionals	0 1
45.	D	Real Conditionals	0 1
46.	A	Complex Sentences	0 1
47.	D	Complex Sentences	0 1
48.	C	Real Conditionals	0 1
49.	B	Complex Sentences	0 1
50.	B	Complex Sentences	0 1
Writing	See p. xii.	Persuasive Writing	0 1 2 3 4

_____ ÷ **54** X **100** = _____
(Student's Total Score)   (Total Possible Points)   (Student's Percent Score)

Student's Name _____

UNIT 5 TEST Answer Key and Tested Skills Chart

ITEM	ANSWER	TESTED SKILL	SCORE (Circle one.)
Listening			
1.	D	Main Idea	0 1
2.	A	Cause and Effect	0 1
3.	A	Making Inferences	0 1
4.	C	Generalizing	0 1
Phonics			
5.	B	Blend *cr*	0 1
6.	D	Blend *fl*	0 1
7.	C	Blend *pl*	0 1
8.	A	Digraphs *ch, tch*	0 1
9.	C	Digraph *wh*	0 1
Spelling			
10.	A	Adding *-er*	0 1
11.	C	Adding *-est*	0 1
12.	B	Adding *-est*	0 1
13.	D	*kn-* Words	0 1
14.	B	*kn-* Words	0 1
Vocabulary			
15.	C	Word Meaning	0 1
16.	C	Word Meaning	0 1
17.	D	Word Meaning	0 1
18.	A	Word Meaning	0 1
19.	B	Context Clues	0 1
20.	A	Context Clues	0 1
21.	A	Context Clues	0 1
22.	C	Context Clues	0 1
Reading			
23.	A	Summarizing	0 1
24.	B	Supporting Details	0 1
25.	C	Making Inferences	0 1
26.	B	Sequence of Events	0 1
27.	C	Taking Notes	0 1
28.	D	Genre	0 1
29.	D	Setting	0 1
30.	C	Making Inferences	0 1
31.	B	Predicting	0 1
32.	C	Genre	0 1
33.	D	Plot	0 1
34.	C	Making Inferences	0 1
35.	B	Summarizing	0 1
36.	B	Hyperbole	0 1
37.	D	Genre	0 1
38.	B	Author's Purpose	0 1
39.	A	Cause and Effect	0 1
40.	B	Supporting Details	0 1
41.	A	Cause and Effect	0 1
42.	D	Cause and Effect	0 1
Grammar			
43.	C	Comparative Adjectives	0 1
44.	B	Superlative Adjectives	0 1
45.	A	Superlative Adjectives	0 1
46.	D	Possessive Pronouns	0 1
47.	A	Possessive Adjectives	0 1
48.	C	Possessive Adjectives	0 1
49.	B	Possessive Pronouns	0 1
50.	B	Comparative Adjectives	0 1
Writing	See p. xii.	Expository Writing	0 1 2 3 4

_____ ÷ **54** X **100** = _____
(Student's Total Score)   (Total Possible Points)   (Student's Percent Score)

Student's Name _____

UNIT 6 TEST Answer Key and Tested Skills Chart

ITEM	ANSWER	TESTED SKILL	SCORE (Circle one.)
Listening			
1.	D	Character	0 1
2.	C	Cause and Effect	0 1
3.	A	Plot	0 1
4.	D	Making Inferences	0 1
Phonics			
5.	A	Digraph *sh*	0 1
6.	C	Digraph *ph*	0 1
7.	B	Digraph *th*	0 1
8.	D	Diphthongs *ou, ow*	0 1
9.	C	Diphthongs *oi, oy*	0 1
Spelling			
10.	C	Words with /th/	0 1
11.	D	Words with /d/	0 1
12.	A	Words with /t/	0 1
13.	C	Adding *-ing*	0 1
14.	A	Adding *-ing*	0 1
Vocabulary			
15.	D	Word Meaning	0 1
16.	B	Word Meaning	0 1
17.	C	Word Meaning	0 1
18.	D	Word Meaning	0 1
19.	C	Context Clues	0 1
20.	D	Context Clues	0 1
21.	A	Context Clues	0 1
22.	B	Context Clues	0 1
Reading			
23.	A	Supporting Details	0 1
24.	A	Supporting Details	0 1
25.	A	Studying Diagrams	0 1
26.	C	Cause and Effect	0 1
27.	C	Supporting Details	0 1
28.	A	Supporting Details	0 1
29.	C	Making Inferences	0 1
30.	D	Hero or Heroine	0 1
31.	B	Conflict	0 1
32.	A	Genre	0 1
33.	B	Narrator	0 1
34.	A	Sequence of Events	0 1
35.	C	Summarizing	0 1
36.	C	Stage Directions	0 1
37.	B	Main Idea	0 1
38.	D	Reading Plays Aloud	0 1
39.	C	Supporting Details	0 1
40.	B	Supporting Details	0 1
41.	D	Cause and Effect	0 1
42.	A	Genre	0 1
Grammar			
43.	D	Quotations	0 1
44.	B	Quotations	0 1
45.	A	Quotations	0 1
46.	D	Quotations	0 1
47.	B	Prepositional Phrases	0 1
48.	C	Prepositional Phrases	0 1
49.	A	Prepositional Phrases	0 1
50.	D	Prepositional Phrases	0 1
Writing	See p. xii.	Writing to Entertain	0 1 2 3 4

_____ ÷ **54** X **100** = _____

(Student's Total Score)   (Total Possible Points)   (Student's Percent Score)

TEST PREPARATION Answer Key and Tested Skills Chart

Taking a Test

ITEM	ANSWER	TESTED SKILL	SCORE (Circle one.)
Vocabulary			
1.	A	Classifying	0 1
2.	A	Classifying	0 1
Phonics			
3.	C	Long *i*	0 1
4.	D	Long *a*	0 1
Grammar			
5.	A	Pronoun Referents	0 1
6.	D	Conjunction *and*	0 1

TEST PREPARATION Answer Key and Tested Skills Chart

Answering Questions About a Passage

ITEM	ANSWER	TESTED SKILL	SCORE (Circle one.)
Reading			
1.	B	Genre	0 1
2.	D	Previewing	0 1
3.	D	Cause and Effect	0 1
4.	B	Drawing Conclusions	0 1

TEST PREPARATION Answer Key and Tested Skills Chart

Answering Multiple-Choice Questions

ITEM	ANSWER	TESTED SKILL	SCORE (Circle one.)
Reading			
1.	C	Plot	0 1
2.	B	Cause and Effect	0 1
3.	C	Supporting Details	0 1
4.	D	Character	0 1

Student's Name _____

TEST PREPARATION Answer Key and Tested Skills Chart
Answering Questions About Meanings of Words

ITEM	ANSWER	TESTED SKILL	SCORE (Circle one.)
Reading			
1.	D	Context Clues	0 1
2.	C	Context Clues	0 1
3.	C	Context Clues/Synonyms	0 1
4.	A	Context Clues/Antonyms	0 1

TEST PREPARATION Answer Key and Tested Skills Chart
Answering Fill-in-the-Blank Items

ITEM	ANSWER	TESTED SKILL	SCORE (Circle one.)
Grammar			
1.	A	Pronoun Referents	0 1
2.	C	Pronoun Referents	0 1
3.	B	Conjunction *and*	0 1
4.	A	Conjunction *or*	0 1
5.	A	Adjectives	0 1
6.	A	Present Tense	0 1

TEST PREPARATION Answer Key and Tested Skills Chart
Responding to a Writing Prompt

ITEM	ANSWER	TESTED SKILL	SCORE (Circle one.)
Writing	See p. xii.	Descriptive Writing	0 1 2 3 4

Shining Star ★B

Diagnostic, Midterm, and Final Tests

Diagnostic Test

LISTENING

DIRECTIONS

Listen to the first passage. Choose the best answer for each item. Then listen to the second passage. Choose the best answer for each item. Circle the letter for the correct answer.

Passage 1: "A Day at the Lake"

1. Tony and his dad go to the—
    A. ocean.
    B. beach.
    C. lake.
    D. river.

2. Tony thinks the best part of the day is—
    A. eating lunch.
    B. catching a fish.
    C. swimming in the water.
    D. listening to his dad's stories.

3. You can tell from the passage that Tony's dad—
    A. is funny.
    B. is a good cook.
    C. does not feel well.
    D. works hard at his job.

4. How does Tony feel at the end of this story?
    A. Happy
    B. Sad
    C. Worried
    D. Sleepy

Passage 2: "Using Lakes for Water, Food, and Fun"

5. Glaciers are—
    A. huge lakes.
    B. large fish.
    C. pieces of ice.
    D. deep valleys.

6. What happened right after the deep valleys were made?
    A. Water filled the valleys.
    B. People skated on the ice.
    C. Glaciers moved slowly.
    D. Birds came to the lakes.

7. Why do birds and land animals come to lakes?
    A. To get away from glaciers
    B. To get drinking water and food
    C. To find a new place to live
    D. To be safe from larger animals

8. This passage tells mostly about—
    A. how to ice-skate on lakes.
    B. ways to have fun on lakes.
    C. ways animals and people use lakes.
    D. why people should not fish in lakes.

PHONICS AND SPELLING

<table>
<tr><td valign="top">

DIRECTIONS

Choose the word with the same sound as the underlined part of the word in the box. Circle the letter for the correct answer.

9. | s<u>a</u>nd |
  A. hard
  B. cake
  C. has
  D. each

10. | t<u>o</u>p |
  A. go
  B. pond
  C. you
  D. stone

11. | f<u>ace</u> |
  A. lake
  B. camp
  C. feet
  D. red

12. | b<u>ir</u>d |
  A. fire
  B. trip
  C. train
  D. hurt

13. | <u>w</u>hite |
  A. where
  B. write
  C. wrap
  D. help

</td><td valign="top">

DIRECTIONS

Find the word that is spelled wrong. Circle the letter for the correct answer.

14. A. can
    B. sea
    C. playn
    D. wet

15. A. hill
    B. five
    C. ride
    D. hygh

16. A. jump
    B. rool
    C. close
    D. stop

17. A. helped
    B. stopped
    C. cryed
    D. played

18. A. wheek
    B. join
    C. west
    D. just

</td></tr>
</table>

GO ON

READING

DIRECTIONS
Read each passage. Then choose the best answer for each item. Circle the letter for the correct answer.

Cleaning Up the Park

The park near the school was full of trash that people dropped on the ground. Mrs. Martin's students wanted to clean up the park. They all went to the park after school. Mrs. Martin gave the students gloves and some bags. "Wear the gloves to keep your hands clean. Put all the trash you find in the bags," she explained.

Mai and Mike picked up empty soda cans, candy wrappers, and other trash. They put all the trash in their bag. "Why don't people use the trash cans in the park?" Mai wondered. Then Mai remembered a time when her mother made signs asking people to throw trash in the neighborhood trash cans and not in the street. "We should put up signs asking people to keep the park clean," Mai said.

"Good idea," said Mike. "Let's tell Mrs. Martin. We can make the signs in art class."

19. Which words from the passage tell you what the park looked like?
    A. Put up signs
    B. Full of trash
    C. Use the trash cans
    D. Keep your hands clean

20. The students probably wanted to clean up the park—
    A. to make the park look nice.
    B. to make the park look messy.
    C. to keep their hands clean.
    D. to make signs in art class.

21. Which is an example of a flashback?
    A. Mai and Mike put trash in a bag.
    B. Mrs. Martin gave gloves to the students.
    C. Mai remembered her mother making signs.
    D. Mai and Mike picked up trash.

22. What will Mai and Mike probably do next?
    A. Play a game in the park
    B. Go to art class and make signs
    C. Drop more trash in the park
    D. Tell Mrs. Martin about making signs

Making Something Old New Again

You can help save the Earth by recycling. When you <u>recycle</u>, you find a new use for something old. For example, you could use an old glass jar to hold your paintbrushes. You could also take the jar to a recycling center. Then other people can make a new jar from your old one. Recycling centers usually recycle glass, metal, plastic, paper, and cardboard. Go to the library or search the Internet to find out how your city recycles old things.

When you recycle and use something again, you make less trash. Less trash helps keep the Earth clean. Recycling also saves the Earth's plants, trees, and other resources. Paper is made from trees. When you recycle old newspapers and school papers, you save trees. So the next time you start to throw something in the trash, ask yourself, "How could I use this again?"

Before you recycle, make sure you clean the inside of jars, cans, and other containers.
Then put your items in separate groups.

23. In this passage, the word <u>recycle</u> means—
   A. to ride your bicycle.
   B. to use something again.
   C. to put things in groups.
   D. to throw things in the trash.

24. Previewing a passage is something you do—
   A. before you read the passage.
   B. as you read the passage.
   C. after you read the passage.
   D. after you take a test about the passage.

25. You can tell that the author of this passage thinks that—
   A. recycling is a good idea.
   B. recycling is not important.
   C. children cannot help the Earth.
   D. people should throw old things away.

26. When you skim the passage, you—
   A. read the passage quickly.
   B. read the passage slowly.
   C. go to the library to find out about recycling.
   D. look up the word <u>recycle</u> in the dictionary.

Vinh saw this poster in the hallway at his school. He told his mother he wanted to go to the Earth Day <u>celebration</u>.

27. What time does the Earth Day celebration start?
   A. 10:00 A.M.
   B. 4:30 P.M.
   C. 6:00 P.M.
   D. 10:00 P.M.

28. Which of these will <u>not</u> be part of the celebration?
   A. Games
   B. Swimming
   C. Music
   D. Food

29. You can tell from the poster that a <u>celebration</u> is—
   A. scary.
   B. fun.
   C. boring.
   D. serious.

30. If you don't understand the information on the poster, the first thing you should do is—
   A. read it again.
   B. skim it quickly.
   C. make your own poster.
   D. think about what will happen next.

GRAMMAR

DIRECTIONS

Read each pair of sentences. Look at the underlined word. Then choose the correct pronoun to complete the second sentence. Circle the letter for the correct answer.

31. My <u>sister</u> did not go to school yesterday. _____ was sick.
    A. She   C. Her
    B. They   D. We

32. We visited my <u>grandparents</u>. We stayed with _____ for two weeks.
    A. it   C. us
    B. them   D. we

DIRECTIONS

Choose the correct word to complete each sentence. Circle the letter for the correct answer.

33. Juan _____ Lucy were both born in Mexico.
    A. but   C. and
    B. or   D. so

34. Ana and her friends _____ to school every day.
    A. will   C. walks
    B. walk   D. walking

35. Step 1 is the _____ thing you do when you make something.
    A. last   C. first
    B. next   D. second

DIRECTIONS

Find the sentence that does not have any mistakes. Circle the letter for the correct answer.

36. A. Who did Tina put her math book?
    B. When did Tina put her math book?
    C. What did Tina put her math book?
    D. Where did Tina put her math book?

37. A. I don't like spiders or snakes.
    B. I don't like spiders than snakes.
    C. I don't like spiders but snakes.
    D. I don't like spiders so snakes.

38. A. Keesha and I wanted to play outside, so it was raining.
    B. Keesha and I wanted to play outside, but it was raining.
    C. Keesha and I wanted to play outside, or it was raining.
    D. Keesha and I wanted to play outside, not it was raining

GO ON

WRITING

WRITING PROMPT

Think of a friend or a family member.

Write a paragraph describing this person. Tell what the person looks like and how the person acts. Be sure to include details in your writing that help readers form a picture of this person. Write on the lines below.

_____

_____

_____

_____

_____

_____

_____

_____

_____

_____

_____

_____

_____

_____

_____

_____

_____

_____

_____

_____

_____

STOP

Midterm Test

LISTENING

DIRECTIONS

Listen to the first passage. Choose the best answer for each item. Then listen to the second passage. Choose the best answer for each item. Circle the letter for the correct answer.

Passage 1: "A Trip to the Mountains"

1. What was the trip called?
- **A.** Mile-High trip
- **B.** Lookout Mountain trip
- **C.** Rocky trip
- **D.** Mother-Daughter trip

2. What can people see from the top of Lookout Mountain?
- **A.** Aunt Mary's cabin
- **B.** The animals at the Denver Zoo
- **C.** The whole city of Denver below
- **D.** The tallest mountain in Canada

3. You can tell from this passage that the person telling the story—
- **A.** did not like to ski.
- **B.** liked the zoo best of all.
- **C.** thinks Ohio is more interesting than Denver.
- **D.** likes visiting a place that is different from Ohio.

4. You can tell that the passage uses the first-person point of view because—
- **A.** it tells about a trip.
- **B.** it uses the pronoun *I*.
- **C.** it tells about Denver.
- **D.** it compares Colorado to Ohio.

Passage 2: "The Rocky Mountains"

5. A mountain chain is—
- **A.** a very tall mountain.
- **B.** a group of mountains.
- **C.** something you use to climb a mountain.
- **D.** something you use to ski down a mountain.

6. The tops of the Rocky Mountains are covered with—
- **A.** snow.
- **B.** forests.
- **C.** lakes.
- **D.** rivers.

7. This passage is—
- **A.** a letter.
- **B.** a play.
- **C.** nonfiction.
- **D.** a poem.

8. You can tell from this passage that the author thinks the Rocky Mountains are—
- **A.** a scary place to drive through.
- **B.** too dangerous for most people.
- **C.** a good place for people to visit.
- **D.** the best place for people to live.

PHONICS AND SPELLING

DIRECTIONS
Choose the word with the same sound as the underlined part of the word in the box. Circle the letter for the correct answer.

9. | tr<u>i</u>be |
   A. wilt
   B. bird
   C. region
   D. five

10. | p<u>o</u>nds |
    A. stone
    B. toads
    C. top
    D. food

11. | cam<u>e</u> |
    A. face
    B. camp
    C. farm
    D. weak

12. | p<u>ar</u>k |
    A. air
    B. arm
    C. work
    D. bear

13. | wh<u>y</u> |
    A. wet
    B. wrong
    C. what
    D. high

DIRECTIONS
Find the word that is spelled wrong. Circle the letter for the correct answer.

14. A. say
    B. can
    C. wet
    D. teers

15. A. hill
    B. time
    C. miel
    D. five

16. A. drum
    B. shop
    C. road
    D. grue

17. A. tried
    B. helpped
    C. relaxed
    D. hoped

18. A. auther
    B. teacher
    C. farmer
    D. poet

GO ON ▶

READING

DIRECTIONS
Read each passage. Then choose the best answer for each item. Circle the letter for the correct answer.

Under the Big Colorado Sky

It is the first day of spring in 1859, but the weather is still cold in the mountains. My brother Jake and I have to ride four more days on horseback to get to Denver. We hope to join other people in Denver who have found gold and become rich!

Today, we stopped near the Colorado River. The river runs through many deep canyons and gorges. Over time, the river slowly wore away soil and rock and made these deep holes in the land.

When it got dark, we used twigs and branches from a tree to build a campfire. Jake cooked corn cakes. We ate them with dried deer meat. Jake and I sang folk songs and watched the stars in the big Colorado sky. We saw a shooting star move in a bright curving line across the sky. I made a wish that we would have luck finding gold in Denver.

19. The brothers are going to Denver—
   A. on vacation.
   B. to find gold.
   C. to sell their gold.
   D. to go home to their family.

20. Which words help you picture a shooting star?
   A. Made a wish
   B. Big Colorado sky
   C. Branches from a tree
   D. Move in a bright curving line

21. Tomorrow, the brothers will probably—
   A. go back home.
   B. keep riding to Denver.
   C. stop to look for gold.
   D. ride a boat down the river.

22. When you identify with a character, you—
   A. think only about other characters.
   B. find only ways that you are different.
   C. find ways that you are alike.
   D. compare the character with others.

John Wesley Powell: Scientist and Explorer

John Wesley Powell spent much of his life learning about nature. Powell was born in Mount Morris, New York, in 1834. As a young boy, Powell was interested in nature. He collected and studied plants, animals, rocks, and shells. He began teaching school when he was eighteen years old to earn money for college. After college, Powell joined the military. He fought in the Civil War and then became a science teacher and an explorer.

Powell wanted to explore the Colorado River. Other people had tried, but they had failed because the river has dangerous waters. Powell talked with Native Americans, hunters, and mountain people who knew the area to learn more about the river. Then, in 1869, he led a group of people on an exploration of the Colorado River. Powell's group was successful. They traveled about 1,000 miles. Powell was the first person to travel that far along the Colorado River. He studied the river and the animals, plants, and rocks near it. He wrote a book about his explorations. Powell died in 1902.

23. Powell was the first person to—
   A. collect plants and rocks.
   B. write a book about exploration.
   C. try to explore the Colorado River.
   D. travel a long way on the Colorado River.

24. This passage is—
   A. a biography.
   B. a poem.
   C. a play.
   D. fiction.

25. You can tell that Powell—
   A. was wealthy.
   B. liked to learn.
   C. moved to Colorado after his trip.
   D. discovered several new plants.

26. When you skim this passage, you—
   A. read it slowly.
   B. read each sentence.
   C. read some sentences.
   D. look up all the words you don't know in a dictionary.

Relief Map of Western United States, Canada, and Mexico

Elevations

Mt. Whitney, California: 14,494 feet above sea level

Mt. Rainier, Washington: 14,410 feet above sea level

Pikes Peak, Colorado: 14,110 feet above sea level

St. Louis, Missouri: 500 feet above sea level

Houston, Texas: 50 feet above sea level

Death Valley, California: 282 feet below sea level

Mt.: mount or mountain

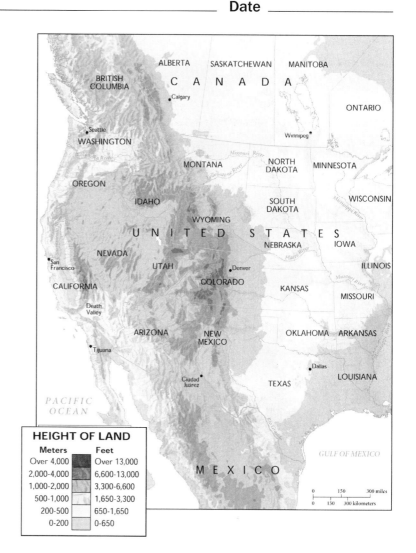

HEIGHT OF LAND

Meters		Feet
Over 4,000		Over 13,000
2,000-4,000		6,600-13,000
1,000-2,000		3,300-6,600
500-1,000		1,650-3,300
200-500		650-1,650
0-200		0-650

Tammy was studying relief maps in school. She learned that a relief map shows an area's height above or below sea level.

27. What is the elevation of Mt. Whitney?
   A. 14,494 feet above sea level
   B. 14,410 feet above sea level
   C. 14,110 feet above sea level
   D. 500 feet above sea level

28. Which of the following places has the lowest elevation?
   A. Pikes Peak
   B. St. Louis
   C. Death Valley
   D. Houston

29. Which of the following places is closest to sea level?
   A. Mt. Rainier
   B. Pikes Peak
   C. St. Louis
   D. Houston

30. According to the map key, which three states have only one general height above sea level?
   A. Montana, Utah, Arizona
   B. Texas, New Mexico, Kansas
   C. New Mexico, Oregon, Nevada
   D. North Dakota, Iowa, Minnesota

GRAMMAR

DIRECTIONS

Read each pair of sentences. Look at the underlined word in the first sentence. Then choose the correct pronoun to complete the second sentence. Circle the letter for the correct answer.

31. The Northwest <u>tribes</u> were good builders. _____ built houses made of cedarwood.
    A. Them   **C.** It
    B. They   **D.** We

32. The Plains tribes collected <u>plants</u>. The tribes used _____ for medicines.
    A. him   **C.** them
    B. us   **D.** you

DIRECTIONS

Choose the word that best completes each sentence. Circle the letter for the correct answer.

33. The explorers used both flat-bottomed boats _____ canoes to go up the river.
    A. and   **C.** not
    B. but   **D.** so

34. An animal _____ oxygen, food, and water.
    A. need   **C.** needing
    B. needs   **D.** will

35. First, the boy caught the fish. Then he cleaned it. _____, he tried to cook it.
    A. First   **C.** Before
    B. Second   **D.** Finally

DIRECTIONS

Find the sentence that does not have any mistakes. Circle the letter for the correct answer.

36. **A.** Who designed the Vietnam Veterans Memorial?
    B. Why designed the Vietnam Veterans Memorial?
    C. Where designed the Vietnam Veterans Memorial?
    D. When designed the Vietnam Veterans Memorial?

37. **A.** Virgil's father wanted to grow lettuce, so he didn't know much about plants.
    B. Virgil's father wanted to grow lettuce, but he didn't know much about plants.
    C. Virgil's father wanted to grow lettuce, or he didn't know much about plants.
    D. Virgil's father wanted to grow lettuce, not he didn't know much about plants.

38. **A.** Virgil went to the garden in the morning, why he watered the lettuce.
    B. Virgil went to the garden in the morning, but he watered the lettuce.
    C. Virgil went to the garden in the morning, or he watered the lettuce.
    D. Virgil went to the garden in the morning, and he watered the lettuce.

WRITING

WRITING PROMPT

Think of a time that you did something that wasn't easy.

Write a story about what happened. Tell what you did and why it was hard. Tell how you felt after you finished it. Be sure to use the first-person point-of-view and the pronoun I. Write on the lines below.

_____

_____

_____

_____

_____

_____

_____

_____

_____

_____

_____

_____

_____

_____

_____

_____

_____

_____

_____

_____

STOP

Final Test

LISTENING

DIRECTIONS

Listen to the first passage. Choose the best answer for each item. Then listen to the second passage. Choose the best answer for each item. Circle the letter for the correct answer.

Passage 1: "Paul Bunyan and Babe"

1. An <u>ox</u> is most like—
   A. a cow.
   B. a tree.
   C. a lake.
   D. an ant.

2. Why did Paul cut down trees?
   A. To make lakes
   B. To get the wood
   C. To make space for towns
   D. To give Babe space to run

3. According to the passage, how did Paul and Babe make the lakes in Minnesota?
   A. They cut down too many trees.
   B. They dug big holes in the ground.
   C. They poured lots of water on the ground.
   D. Their footsteps made big holes in the ground.

4. Which sentence from the passage tells you that the passage is a tall tale?
   A. An ox is an animal somewhat like a cow.
   B. Now Minnesota is called the "Land of 10,000 Lakes."
   C. When Paul grew up, he traveled around the country.
   D. People said that Paul could eat forty bowls of soup—just as a snack!

Passage 2: "Trees in North America"

5. Why did people in North America first cut down trees?
   A. To recycle paper
   B. To get food to eat
   C. To make space for new trees
   D. To make space for roads, farms, and towns

6. Wood pulp is used—
   A. to make paper.
   B. to build houses.
   C. for heating houses.
   D. for cooking food.

7. Today, many people worry about trees because they think—
   A. trees make the air dirty.
   B. Earth has too many trees.
   C. too many trees are being cut down.
   D. trees are not good for making things.

8. Another good title for this passage is—
   A. "Different Kinds of Trees."
   B. "Using Trees to Build Roads."
   C. "Take Care of Earth's Trees."
   D. "How to Build Your Own House."

PHONICS AND SPELLING

DIRECTIONS

Choose the word with the same sound as the underlined part of the word in the box. Circle the letter for the correct answer.

9. | ab<u>o</u>ve |
   - **A.** ant
   - **B.** east
   - **C.** other
   - **D.** playing

10. | day<u>s</u> |
   - **A.** hands
   - **B.** place
   - **C.** yes
   - **D.** glass

11. | <u>fl</u>oor |
   - **A.** feel
   - **B.** fall
   - **C.** flat
   - **D.** look

12. | ea<u>ch</u> |
   - **A.** school
   - **B.** face
   - **C.** rock
   - **D.** coach

13. | h<u>ow</u> |
   - **A.** show
   - **B.** house
   - **C.** noise
   - **D.** award

DIRECTIONS

Find the word that is spelled wrong. Circle the letter for the correct answer.

14.
   - **A.** middel
   - **B.** travel
   - **C.** about
   - **D.** little

15.
   - **A.** boats
   - **B.** classes
   - **C.** leaves
   - **D.** babyes

16.
   - **A.** heaviest
   - **B.** happyer
   - **C.** angrier
   - **D.** funniest

17.
   - **A.** knot
   - **B.** knee
   - **C.** nife
   - **D.** know

18.
   - **A.** growing
   - **B.** winning
   - **C.** trying
   - **D.** driveing

GO ON

Final Test/Phonics and Spelling

Name _____   Date _____

READING

DIRECTIONS

Read each passage. Then choose the best answer for each item. Circle the letter for the correct answer.

E-Mail Message to Grandma

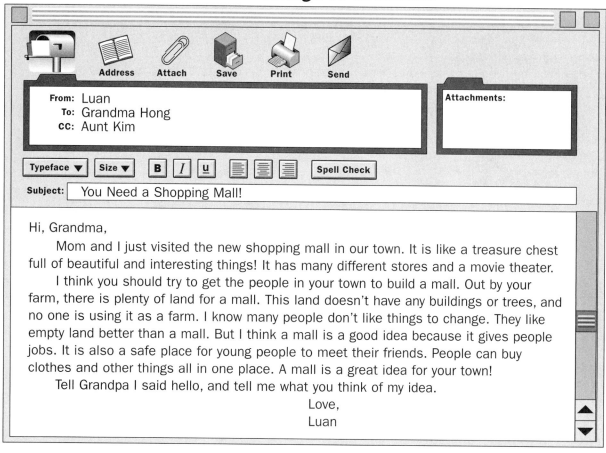

From: Luan
To: Grandma Hong
cc: Aunt Kim

Subject: You Need a Shopping Mall!

Hi, Grandma,

Mom and I just visited the new shopping mall in our town. It is like a treasure chest full of beautiful and interesting things! It has many different stores and a movie theater.

I think you should try to get the people in your town to build a mall. Out by your farm, there is plenty of land for a mall. This land doesn't have any buildings or trees, and no one is using it as a farm. I know many people don't like things to change. They like empty land better than a mall. But I think a mall is a good idea because it gives people jobs. It is also a safe place for young people to meet their friends. People can buy clothes and other things all in one place. A mall is a great idea for your town!

Tell Grandpa I said hello, and tell me what you think of my idea.

Love,
Luan

---

19. Where does Grandma Hong live?
   A. With Luan
   B. On a farm
   C. Near a mall
   D. In Luan's town

20. The writer of the message says the mall "is like a treasure chest full of beautiful and interesting things!" This sentence is an example of a—
   A. conflict.
   B. simile.
   C. dialogue.
   D. stage direction.

21. What is one reason that Luan thinks a mall is a good idea?
   A. Everyone likes to shop.
   B. A mall gives people jobs.
   C. No one wants the town to stay the same.
   D. People like a mall better than empty land.

22. When you use your own experience to understand this message, you—
   A. guess what Grandma will think.
   B. skim the title and some sentences.
   C. ask yourself what you like and don't like about a mall near you.
   D. get more information about malls.

Shopping Malls

The first shopping mall opened in Kansas City, Missouri, in 1922. Before this mall, people shopped in different buildings. Today, many people shop at shopping malls. A shopping mall usually has many stores in one large building or in a group of joined buildings. Most malls have stores that sell things, and some have places to eat. There are also <u>services</u>, which are places where people do things for you, such as cut your hair. Some malls have movie theaters and game rooms.

The world's largest mall is in Alberta, Canada. This mall has eleven large stores, more than 800 smaller stores, and 110 places to eat! For fun, visitors can ice-skate on the indoor ice rink, play in an indoor water park, or visit animals at a zoo. This mall even has a hotel for people who want to stay more than one day.

Many people think malls are great because you can do all your shopping in one place. Other people think malls are ugly and too big. They like the old way of shopping better.

23. This passage is—
    A. fiction.
    B. nonfiction.
    C. a biography.
    D. an e-mail message.

24. What important event happened in 1922?
    A. The first shopping mall opened.
    B. The first indoor water park opened.
    C. The first movie theater was built inside a mall.
    D. The world's largest shopping mall was built.

25. <u>Services</u> are places—
    A. that show movies.
    B. where you play games.
    C. where you can go to eat.
    D. where things are done for you.

26. Which of these sentences best summarizes the last paragraph?
    A. Malls are ugly and too big.
    B. Some people like malls, but others do not.
    C. You can do all your shopping in one place at a mall.
    D. Just about everyone loves to shop at big shopping malls.

Name _____ Date _____

Jenny found this directory on the second floor of the East Town Mall. A directory shows a diagram of where places are located. Each place is marked with a number, and a list shows the names of places and their numbers. The words "You Are Here" show where you are when you are looking at the directory, so you can find other places in the mall.

East Town Mall, second floor

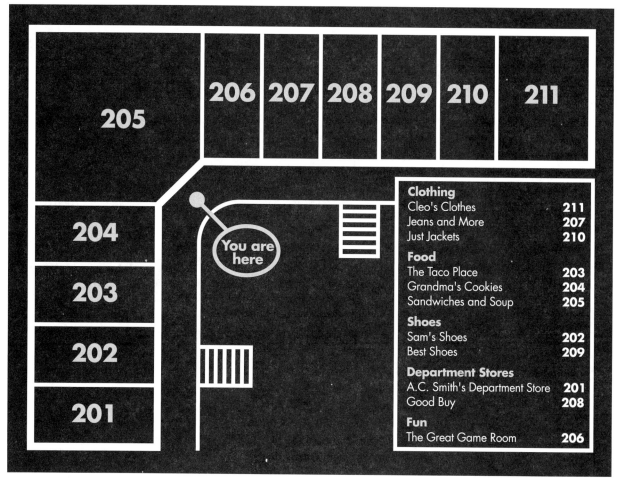

27. How many clothing stores are on the second floor of East Town Mall?
- **A.** One
- **B.** Three
- **C.** Four
- **D.** You can't tell from the directory.

28. What number is Sam's Shoes?
- **A.** 201
- **B.** 202
- **C.** 205
- **D.** 209

29. What food can you get at the place marked 204?
- **A.** Tacos
- **B.** Cookies
- **C.** Sandwiches
- **D.** Soup

30. The words "You Are Here" show that the directory is in front of—
- **A.** store 201.
- **B.** store 203.
- **C.** store 206.
- **D.** store 205.

Name _____ Date _____

GRAMMAR

DIRECTIONS
Choose the word or words that best complete each sentence. Circle the letter for the correct answer.

31. If we save energy and recycle, we _____ Earth.
  A. will   **C.** help
  B. helped   **D.** helping

32. The Mexican army was _____ than the Texas army.
  A. big   **C.** biggest
  B. bigger   **D.** most big

33. Swift Runner raced the old woman _____ very long legs.
  A. in   **C.** at
  B. with   **D.** to

DIRECTIONS
Read each pair of sentences. Choose the word that best completes the second sentence. Circle the letter for the correct answer.

34. Her horse is brown. _____ is black.
  A. Mine   **C.** Your
  B. My   **D.** Our

35. Their ranch is big. _____ ranch is small.
  A. Mine   **C.** Theirs
  B. Yours   **D.** Our

DIRECTIONS
Find the sentence that does not have any mistakes. Circle the letter for the correct answer.

36. A. When Shirley shut both eyes.
  B. Shirley shut both eyes, the principal laughed.
  C. When Shirley shut both eyes, the principal laughed.
  D. When Shirley shut both eyes the principal laughed.

37. A. Papa's cotton crop this year is the best crop ever.
  B. Papa's cotton crop this year is the most best crop ever.
  C. Papa's cotton crop this year is the bestest crop ever.
  D. Papa's cotton crop this year is the better crop ever.

38. A. I must save my people Glooskap said.
  B. "I must save my people," Glooskap said.
  C. "I must save my people," Glooskap said."
  D. I must save my people, "Glooskap said.

Final Test/Grammar

WRITING

> ## WRITING PROMPT
> Think of something funny that happened with your friends or family.
> Write a skit about what happened. Your skit should have two or more characters, dialogue for each character, and stage directions. Write on the lines below.

_____

_____

_____

_____

_____

_____

_____

_____

_____

_____

_____

_____

_____

_____

_____

_____

_____

_____

_____

_____

STOP

Shining Star ★ B

Part Tests

UNIT 1 Part 1 Test

VOCABULARY

DIRECTIONS
Look at the word webs. Find the missing word. Circle the letter for the correct answer.

1. Find the missing word.

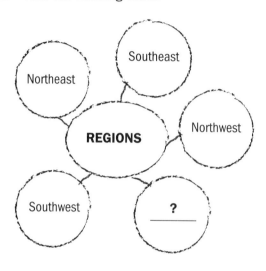

A. rivers	**C.** Plains
B. Sioux	**D.** canoes

2. Find the missing word.

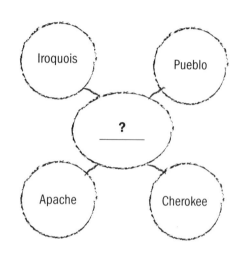

A. states	**C.** climates
B. tribes	**D.** countries

DIRECTIONS
Choose the word that best completes each sentence. Circle the letter for the correct answer.

3. Land, water, and air are all part of Earth's _____.
A. arid	**C.** irrigate
B. nomad	**D.** environment

4. The Pueblo learned to _____ crops with little water.
A. arid	**C.** climate
B. irrigate	**D.** environment

5. Native Americans who followed buffalo herds from place to place were _____.
A. nomads	**C.** climates
B. regions	**D.** environments

6. The Southwest has a hot and dry _____.
A. tribe	**C.** climate
B. nomad	**D.** irrigate

GO ON

READING: "The First Americans"

DIRECTIONS
Choose the best answer for each item. Circle the letter for the correct answer.

7. "The First Americans" is—
   A. a song.
   B. a poem.
   C. fiction.
   D. nonfiction.

8. Some scientists think that the first Americans migrated from—
   A. Asia.
   B. Africa.
   C. Europe.
   D. Australia.

9. Why did the Pueblo perform the Snake Ceremony?
   A. To make snakes leave their villages
   B. To get snakes to come to their villages
   C. To bring rain and make their crops grow
   D. To celebrate the building of a new house

10. Why did most of the Southeast tribes move west?
    A. They wanted to live near European settlers.
    B. There was not enough food in the Southeast.
    C. They wanted to hunt buffalo in the Southwest.
    D. European settlers forced them to leave their land.

11. Why did the author write "The First Americans"?
    A. To describe the lives of Native Americans today
    B. To tell about Native Americans who lived long ago
    C. To explain why the United States is a good place to live
    D. To describe interesting places to visit in the United States

12. When you preview a passage, the titles and headings help you—
    A. find facts about the passage.
    B. find examples of alliteration.
    C. predict what the passage will be about.
    D. understand words you don't know.

READING: "This Land Is Your Land" and "Roll On, Columbia"

DIRECTIONS
Choose the best answer for each item. Circle the letter for the correct answer.

"This Land Is Your Land"

13. "This Land Is Your Land" is—
   A. a song.
   B. an essay.
   C. a story.
   D. an informational text.

14. Which words from the passage are examples of alliteration?
   A. Dust clouds rolling
   B. Her diamond deserts
   C. That ribbon of highway
   D. The gulfstream waters

"Roll On, Columbia"

15. What is "Roll On, Columbia" mostly about?
   A. A famous songwriter
   B. Famous rivers in the world
   C. Traveling in a canoe on a river
   D. A powerful river in the Northwest

16. You can tell from the two passages that Woody Guthrie—
   A. did not like to travel.
   B. did not visit the places he wrote about.
   C. thought of the United States as a beautiful country.
   D. thought of California and New York as the best states.

GRAMMAR AND WRITING

DIRECTIONS

Read each pair of sentences. Look at the underlined word in the first sentence. Then choose the correct pronoun to complete the second sentence. Circle the letter for the correct answer.

17. Many <u>tribes</u> lived in the Northeast. _____ made tools and canoes.
    - **A.** It
    - **B.** He
    - **C.** She
    - **D.** They

18. The <u>Southwest</u> does not get much rain. _____ is a hot, arid place.
    - **A.** It
    - **B.** We
    - **C.** You
    - **D.** They

19. The Makah people built big <u>canoes</u>. The tribe used _____ to hunt whales in the ocean.
    - **A.** it
    - **B.** her
    - **C.** him
    - **D.** them

20. We gave my <u>grandfather</u> some birthday presents. I bought _____ a book about Woody Guthrie.
    - **A.** her
    - **B.** him
    - **C.** you
    - **D.** them

DIRECTIONS

Find the sentence that has no mistakes. Circle the letter for the correct sentence.

21. **A.** Many Native American tribes live in the Southwest.
    B. Many Native American tribes live in the Southwest
    C. many Native American tribes live in the Southwest.
    D. Many Native American tribes live in the Southwest?

22. **A.** The desert has hot a climate.
    B. The desert has a climate hot.
    C. The desert has a hot climate.
    D. The desert hot has a climate.

UNIT 1 Part 2 Test

VOCABULARY

DIRECTIONS

Look at the word webs. Find the missing word or words. Circle the letter for the correct answer.

1. Find the missing word or words.

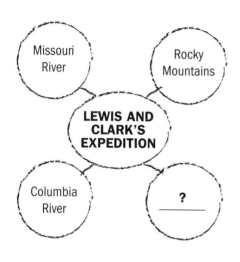

2. Find the missing word.

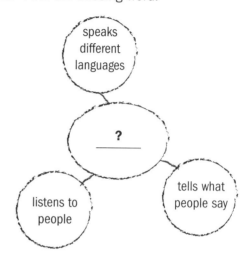

A. canoes	**C.** Sacagawea
B. moccasins	**D.** Pacific Ocean

A. explorer	**C.** moccasins
B. interpreter	**D.** recognized

DIRECTIONS

Choose the word that best completes each sentence. Circle the letter for the correct answer.

3. The Minnetaree took Sacagawea to a village far away after they _____ her.
  A. lost   **C.** kidnapped
  B. traded   **D.** recognized

4. Soft leather shoes are called _____.
  A. canoes   **C.** interpreters
  B. moccasins   **D.** expeditions

5. When Sacagawea heard her brother speak, she _____ him.
  A. traveled   **C.** kidnapped
  B. captured   **D.** recognized

6. The explorers wanted to _____ their things to get horses from the Shoshone.
  A. trade   **C.** explore
  B. watch   **D.** kidnapped

GO ON ▶

READING: from *River to Tomorrow*

DIRECTIONS
Choose the best answer for each item. Circle the letter for the correct answer.

7. Who was Sacagawea?
   A. The chief of the United States
   B. The chief of the Shoshone people
   C. A captain who led an expedition
   D. A Shoshone woman who helped Lewis and Clark

8. Why did the explorers want to find the Shoshone?
   A. To get maps from the Shoshone
   B. To get horses from the Shoshone
   C. To return Sacagawea to her people
   D. To learn about the Shoshone language

9. The passage says, "They ached from the piercing prickly pear thorns that tore their clothes and flesh." These words help you visualize—
   A. how long the journey was.
   B. how easy the journey was.
   C. how treacherous the rapids were.
   D. how hard the journey was.

10. What is a flashback?
   A. The place where the story takes place
   B. Something the character did or felt in the past
   C. A guess about what will happen next in the story
   D. A word with the same beginning sound as another word

11. Why was Sacagawea filled with peace at the end of the story?
   A. She enjoyed the journey.
   B. She found her child, Pomp.
   C. She found her home and family.
   D. She did not feel hungry anymore.

12. Historical fiction tells about—
   A. only real things.
   B. only imaginary things.
   C. both real things and imaginary things.
   D. things that will happen in the future.

READING: "Reading a Relief Map"

DIRECTIONS
Choose the best answer for each item. Circle the letter for the correct answer.

13. A relief map shows—
- **A.** how many people live in a region.
- **B.** the elevation of different regions.
- **C.** things people can do in different regions.
- **D.** places where you can get help for problems.

14. On a relief map, you use a key—
- **A.** to open locked doors.
- **B.** to find the answer to a problem.
- **C.** to see how high the land is above sea level.
- **D.** to find the location of large buildings in a city.

15. A scale on a map helps you figure out—
- **A.** the distance between places.
- **B.** how much something weighs.
- **C.** how high the land is above sea level.
- **D.** whether the land has hills, mountains, or plains.

16. Which of these has the highest elevation?
- **A.** Sea
- **B.** Hill
- **C.** Plain
- **D.** Mountain

GRAMMAR AND WRITING

DIRECTIONS
Choose the word that best completes each sentence. Circle the letter for the correct answer.

17. Lewis _____ Clark were the two leaders of the expedition.
    - **A.** so
    - **B.** or
    - **C.** but
    - **D.** and

18. The explorers had to choose to go on _____ to go back.
    - **A.** so
    - **B.** or
    - **C.** but
    - **D.** and

19. Sacagawea hugged her brother _____ cried.
    - **A.** or
    - **B.** so
    - **C.** and
    - **D.** but

20. Captain Lewis did not speak the Shoshone _____ Minnetaree language.
    - **A.** or
    - **B.** so
    - **C.** and
    - **D.** but

DIRECTIONS
Find the sentence that has no mistakes. Circle the letter for the correct sentence.

21. **A.** Did you like reading about Sacagawea
    - **B.** Did you like reading about Sacagawea?
    - **C.** Did you like reading about Sacagawea!
    - **D.** did you like reading about Sacagawea.

22. **A.** tina and i liked reading about Sacagawea.
    - **B.** tina and I liked reading about Sacagawea.
    - **C.** Tina and i liked reading about Sacagawea.
    - **D.** Tina and I liked reading about Sacagawea.

STOP

UNIT 2 Part 1 Test

VOCABULARY

DIRECTIONS

Look at the word webs. Find the missing word or words. Circle the letter for the correct answer.

1.   Find the missing word.

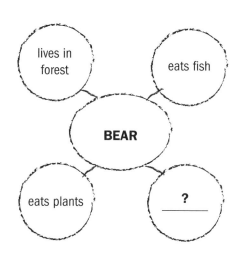

2.   Find the missing word.

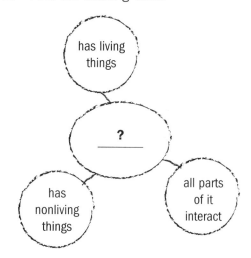

A.	omnivore	**C.**	carnivore
B.	herbivore	**D.**	decomposer

A.	sunlight	**C.**	ecosystem
B.	organism	**D.**	carnivore

DIRECTIONS

Choose the word that best completes each sentence. Circle the letter for the correct answer.

3.   Animals that eat only plants are _____.
  A. carnivores   **C.** omnivores
  B. herbivores   **D.** scavengers

4.   Animals that eat only other animals are _____.
  A. carnivores   **C.** omnivores
  B. herbivores   **D.** scavengers

5.   A tree and a mouse are living things, so they are _____.
  A. plants   **C.** carnivores
  B. animals   **D.** organisms

6.   Snakes and lizards _____ with one another because they live close together in the desert.
  A. eat   **C.** organism
  B. interact   **D.** reproduce

READING: "Ecosystems: The Systems of Nature"

DIRECTIONS
Choose the best answer for each item. Circle the letter for the correct answer.

7. "Ecosystems: The Systems of Nature" is—
   A. a poem.
   B. a song.
   C. historical fiction.
   D. an informational text.

8. How are a child, a tree, and an insect alike?
   A. All are large.
   B. All are small.
   C. All are organisms.
   D. All are carnivores.

9. What is a habitat?
   A. A baby that two animals create
   B. A place where an organism lives
   C. A group of animals that are alike
   D. A kind of plant that an animal eats

10. Which of these is <u>not</u> part of an oak tree's ecosystem?
    A. Plants that live near the oak tree
    B. The soil that the oak tree grows in
    C. The animals that live in the oak tree
    D. Other trees that live far from the oak tree

11. A food chain always begins with—
    A. plants.
    B. decomposers.
    C. big consumers.
    D. small consumers.

12. Reading a text quickly is called—
    A. rhyming.
    B. predicting.
    C. skimming.
    D. visualizing.

READING: "The Bat" and "The Snake"

DIRECTIONS
Choose the best answer for each item. Circle the letter for the correct answer.

"The Bat"

13. Which words from "The Bat" rhyme?
  A. Hat, head
  B. Night, light
  C. Attic, house
  D. Mice, wings

14. In the poem, the poet compares a bat to—
  A. a hat.
  B. a tree.
  C. an attic.
  D. a mouse.

"The Snake"

15. The poet uses the words spotted shaft to describe—
  A. what a snake eats.
  B. how a snake looks.
  C. how a snake moves.
  D. where a snake lives.

16. How does the speaker in the poem feel when meeting a snake?
  A. Bored
  B. Happy
  C. Nervous
  D. Friendly

GO ON

GRAMMAR AND WRITING

DIRECTIONS
Choose the word or words that best complete each sentence. Circle the letter for the correct answer.

17. Snakes _____ quickly through the grass.
- **A.** move
- **B.** moves
- **C.** moving
- **D.** to move

18. A bat and a snake _____ insects.
- **A.** eat
- **B.** eats
- **C.** eated
- **D.** eating

19. A fish _____ in water.
- **A.** life
- **B.** live
- **C.** lives
- **D.** living

20. She _____ birds in her backyard.
- **A.** watch
- **B.** watches
- **C.** watching
- **D.** to watch

DIRECTIONS
Find the sentence that has no mistakes. Circle the letter for the correct sentence.

21.
- **A.** Many bats live in the United states and mexico.
- **B.** Many bats live in the United States and mexico.
- **C.** Many bats live in the united states and Mexico.
- **D.** Many bats live in the United States and Mexico.

22.
- **A.** Emily dickinson wrote almost 2,000 poems.
- **B.** Emily Dickinson wrote almost 2,000 poems.
- **C.** Emily Dickinson wrote almost 2,000 Poems.
- **D.** emily dickinson wrote almost 2,000 poems.

STOP

UNIT 2 Part 2 Test

VOCABULARY

DIRECTIONS
Look at the word webs. Find the missing word. Circle the letter for the correct answer.

1. Find the missing word.

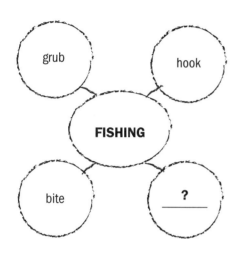

2. Find the missing word.

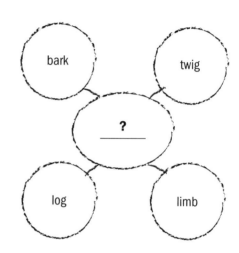

A. log	**C.** bark
B. line	**D.** moss

A. tree	**C.** bank
B. fish	**D.** game

DIRECTIONS
Choose the word that best completes each sentence. Circle the letter for the correct answer.

3. Sam sat on the _____ of the stream.
   A. line   **C.** grub
   B. bark   **D.** bank

4. Sam used string to make a _____ and then tied a hook on it.
   A. line   **C.** bark
   B. grub   **D.** bank

5. Sam put a white, wiggling _____ on his hook.
   A. bite   **C.** grub
   B. bark   **D.** bank

6. People use traps to catch _____ in the forest.
   A. bank   **C.** grub
   B. bark   **D.** game

READING: from *My Side of the Mountain*

DIRECTIONS
Choose the best answer for each item. Circle the letter for the correct answer.

7. What did Sam make with twigs and bark?
   A. A bed
   B. A line
   C. A trap
   D. A fishhook

8. Which problem did Sam have when he tried to catch a fish?
   A. His hook broke.
   B. He fell in the stream.
   C. He could not find a grub.
   D. He could not catch a fish.

9. Which problem did Sam have when he tried to build a fire?
   A. He did not find any dry wood.
   B. He could not get the fire to start.
   C. He did not have anything to start a fire with.
   D. The wind and rain kept putting his fire out.

10. Which sentence from the passage is an example of personification?
   A. I chopped away until I found a cold white grub.
   B. It wasn't hard to find a pretty spot along that stream.
   C. I remembered about old logs and all the sleeping stages of insects that are in it.
   D. Suddenly, the string came to life and rode back and forth and around in a circle.

11. You can tell from what Sam did that he—
   A. usually quits when he has a problem.
   B. likes to spend time with other people.
   C. enjoys learning how to do new things.
   D. always does something right the first time.

12. When you try to understand how Sam feels and acts, you are—
   A. visualizing a place.
   B. skimming a passage.
   C. previewing a passage.
   D. identifying with a character.

Name _____ Date _____

READING: "Water and Living Things"

DIRECTIONS
Choose the best answer for each item. Circle the letter for the correct answer.

13. Most of the water on Earth is in—
   A. ponds.
   B. rivers.
   C. oceans.
   D. streams.

14. The water cycle describes—
   A. how plants use water.
   B. how water moves from one place to another.
   C. the names for the different parts of the ocean.
   D. the difference between salt water and fresh water.

15. What happens when water evaporates?
   A. It changes into water vapor.
   B. It changes into liquid water drops.
   C. It falls back to Earth as rain, snow, sleet, or hail.
   D. It fills small cracks and spaces under the ground.

16. An expository text—
   A. has stanzas and uses rhyme.
   B. tells about imaginary people.
   C. tells about the author's personal experience.
   D. explains something or tells how something works.

GRAMMAR AND WRITING

DIRECTIONS
Choose the word that best completes each sentence. Circle the letter for the correct answer.

17. Sam used his knife _____.
- **A.** care
- **B.** careful
- **C.** carefully
- **D.** carefuller

18. Fish _____ gather in calm water.
- **A.** usual
- **B.** usually
- **C.** usualled
- **D.** usualing

19. Sam ran _____ through the forest, picking up firewood.
- **A.** quickly
- **B.** quicker
- **C.** quickest
- **D.** quicken

20. The wind blew _____ through the trees.
- **A.** loud
- **B.** louding
- **C.** loudest
- **D.** loudly

DIRECTIONS
Find the sentence that has no mistakes. Circle the letter for the correct sentence.

21. **A.** You use always dry wood to make a fire.
   B. You always use dry wood to make a fire.
   C. Always you use dry wood to make a fire.
   D. You use always dry wood to make a fire.

22. **A.** You never leave your fire burning when you are not at camp.
   B. You leave never your fire burning when you are not at camp.
   C. You leave your fire burning never when you are not at camp.
   D. Never you leave your fire burning when you are not at camp.

UNIT 3 Part 1 Test

VOCABULARY

DIRECTIONS
Look at the word webs. Find the missing word. Circle the letter for the correct answer.

1. Find the missing word.

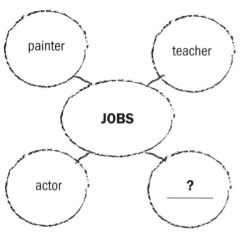

A. money	**C.** astronaut
B. ordinary	**D.** autobiography

2. Find the missing word.

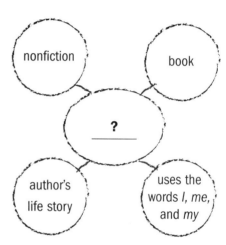

A. fiction	**C.** biography
B. astronaut	**D.** autobiography

DIRECTIONS
Choose the word or words that best complete each sentence. Circle the letter for the correct answer.

3. Naomi Shihab Nye's poems are often about _____ people who live like everyone else.
    A. strang   **C.** ordinary
    B. exciting   **D.** astronaut

4. Nye's poems show different people's opinions, or _____.
    A. astronauts   **C.** points of view
    B. distributes   **D.** autobiographies

5. The World Wide Web is used to _____ information to people around the world.
    A. distribute   **C.** remember
    B. astronaut   **D.** traditional

6. Frida Kahlo loved her culture and wore _____ Mexican clothes and jewelry.
    A. brave   **C.** serious
    B. weak   **D.** traditional

READING: "Success Stories"

DIRECTIONS
Choose the best answer for each item. Circle the letter for the correct answer.

7. "Success Stories" is a group of—
   A. plays.
   B. poems.
   C. biographies.
   D. fictional stories.

8. Frida Kahlo was a famous Mexican—
   A. doctor.
   B. painter.
   C. astronaut.
   D. photographer.

9. You can tell from the passage that Naomi Shihab Nye—
   A. enjoys writing about different cultures.
   B. likes writing nonfiction better than fiction.
   C. wishes her family had stayed in Jerusalem.
   D. writes only about Arab Americans like herself.

10. You can tell from the passage that Christopher Reeve—
    A. thinks people should not ride horses.
    B. can no longer work because of the accident.
    C. does not enjoy learning about new things.
    D. keeps trying to do things even if they are difficult.

11. What was special about Dr. Mae Jemison's trip on the *Endeavour*?
    A. There were seven astronauts on the space shuttle.
    B. It was the first time a woman traveled into space.
    C. It was the first time people on Earth saw a spaceflight.
    D. It was the first time an African-American woman went into space.

12. How did Tim Berners-Lee's invention of the World Wide Web help people?
    A. It made the Internet smaller.
    B. It put more information on the Internet.
    C. It made it easier to get information on the Internet.
    D. It made computers less expensive and easier to use.

READING: "An Interview with Naomi Shihab Nye"

DIRECTIONS
Choose the best answer for each item. Circle the letter for the correct answer.

13. What usually happens in an interview?
- **A.** Someone sings a song.
- **B.** Actors read words aloud.
- **C.** Writers use words that rhyme.
- **D.** Someone asks a person questions.

14. When did Nye start writing poems?
- **A.** When she was a little girl
- **B.** When she was in high school
- **C.** During a writing class in college
- **D.** After she graduated from college

15. How does Nye feel about the three main places she has lived?
- **A.** The three places are much alike.
- **B.** Each place is special and important.
- **C.** It is best to live in one place your whole life.
- **D.** Jerusalem is the most interesting place to live.

16. Which of the following is <u>not</u> something Nye thinks young writers should do?
- **A.** Do a lot of reading.
- **B.** Discuss your writing with others.
- **C.** Wait until your writing is really good before you share it.
- **D.** Start your own writing circle of friends who enjoy writing.

Name _____ Date _____

GRAMMAR AND WRITING

DIRECTIONS

Read each sentence. Choose the word that best completes each sentence. Circle the letter for the correct answer.

17. _____ did Frida Kahlo paint her first self-portrait?
    A. Who   **C.** When
    B. What   **D.** Didn't

18. _____ wrote the autobiography *Still Me*?
    A. Why   **C.** When
    B. Who   **D.** Where

19. _____ did Dr. Mae Jemison do on the *Endeavour*?
    A. What   **C.** When
    B. Why   **D.** Where

20. _____ Tim Berners-Lee invent the World Wide Web?
    A. Why   **C.** Where
    B. Who   **D.** Didn't

DIRECTIONS

Find the sentence that has no mistakes. Circle the letter for the correct sentence.

21. **A.** Where did Naomi Shihab Nye live in Jerusalem
    B. Where did Naomi Shihab Nye live in Jerusalem!
    C. Where did Naomi Shihab Nye live in Jerusalem.
    D. Where did Naomi Shihab Nye live in Jerusalem?

22. **A.** Why Dr. Mae Jemison become an astronaut?
    B. Why do Dr. Mae Jemison become an astronaut?
    C. Why did Dr. Mae Jemison become an astronaut?
    D. Did why Dr. Mae Jemison become an astronaut?

UNIT 3 Part 2 Test

VOCABULARY

DIRECTIONS
Look at the word webs. Find the missing word. Circle the letter for the correct answer.

1. Find the missing word.

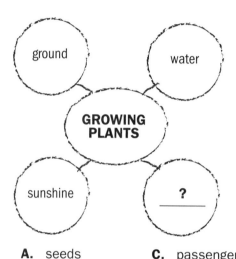

    A. seeds   **C.** passengers
    B. lockets   **D.** coincidences

2. Find the missing word.

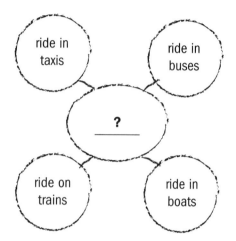

    A. ground   **C.** passengers
    B. plantations   **D.** coincidences

DIRECTIONS
Choose the word that best completes each sentence. Circle the letter for the correct answer.

3. It was a _____ that Virgil found the locket in the trash, since he wasn't looking for it.
    A. plan   **C.** plantation
    B. package   **D.** coincidence

4. The sun was so hot that the plants started to _____ and die.
    A. wilt   **C.** water
    B. pour   **D.** ground

5. Virgil opened the _____ of lettuce seeds.
    A. ground   **C.** passenger
    B. package   **D.** coincidence

6. The farmer grew cotton on his large _____.
    A. seed   **C.** plantation
    B. passenger   **D.** coincidence

GO ON ▶

READING: from *Seedfolks*

DIRECTIONS
Choose the best answer for each item. Circle the letter for the correct answer.

7. The chapter from *Seedfolks* is most like a—
   A. play.
   B. myth.
   C. short story.
   D. biography.

8. Who is the first-person narrator in the chapter from *Seedfolks*?
   A. Virgil
   B. Miss Fleck
   C. Virgil's dad
   D. The girl in the locket

9. What is the chapter from *Seedfolks* mostly about?
   A. Driving a taxi
   B. Finding a locket
   C. Trying to sell lettuce
   D. Trying to grow lettuce

10. Why does Virgil's dad want a garden?
    A. To make money
    B. To feed his family
    C. To grow food for relatives in Haiti
    D. So he can spend more time with Virgil

11. The lettuce wilts and dies because—
    A. bugs eat the plants.
    B. it is too hot outside.
    C. Virgil washed the seeds out of place.
    D. Virgil didn't give them enough water.

12. If you don't understand why Virgil gets mad at his dad, you should—
    A. read more quickly.
    B. preview the chapter to find main ideas.
    C. keep reading to the end of the chapter.
    D. reread the part of the story before Virgil gets angry.

GO ON

READING: "How Seeds and Plants Grow"

DIRECTIONS
Choose the best answer for each item. Circle the letter for the correct answer.

13. Which of these is <u>not</u> part of a seed?
- **A.** Embryo
- **B.** Seed coat
- **C.** Stored food
- **D.** Photosynthesis

14. What does the seed coat do?
- **A.** It keeps the embryo warm.
- **B.** It helps a plant make its own food.
- **C.** It makes young plants grow straight.
- **D.** It keeps the stored food from drying out.

15. What is the first thing that happens during germination?
- **A.** The seed coat breaks open.
- **B.** The embryo starts to grow.
- **C.** The first leaves appear on the stem.
- **D.** The stem breaks above the ground.

16. What happens after the first leaves appear on the stem?
- **A.** The seed coat breaks open.
- **B.** The roots start to grow downward.
- **C.** The plant starts to make its own food.
- **D.** The embryo starts to use its stored food.

GRAMMAR AND WRITING

DIRECTIONS

Choose the word that best completes each sentence. Circle the letter for the correct answer.

17. Virgil dug in the ground, _____ he found a locket.
- **A.** or
- **B.** but
- **C.** and
- **D.** because

18. Virgil washed the seeds out of place, _____ the lettuce came up in wavy lines.
- **A.** so
- **B.** or
- **C.** for
- **D.** but

19. You can plant lettuce seeds in the spring, _____ you can plant them in the fall.
- **A.** so
- **B.** or
- **C.** for
- **D.** because

20. Virgil's eyes opened wide, _____ he had never watched an adult lie before.
- **A.** or
- **B.** so
- **C.** and
- **D.** for

Find the sentence that has no mistakes. Circle the letter for the correct sentence.

21. **A.** Virgil's father wants to sell the lettuce but the lettuce wilts.
   B. Virgil's father wants to sell the lettuce, but the lettuce wilts.
   C. Virgil's father wants to sell the lettuce but, the lettuce wilts.
   D. Virgil's father wants to sell the lettuce, but, the lettuce wilts.

22. **A.** A seed may grow right away or it may take years to grow.
   B. A seed may grow right away or, it may take years to grow.
   C. A seed may grow right away, or it may take years to grow.
   D. A seed may grow right away, or, it may take years to grow.

STOP

UNIT 4 Part 1 Test

VOCABULARY

DIRECTIONS
Look at the word webs. Find the missing word or words. Circle the letter for the correct answer.

1. Find the missing word or words.

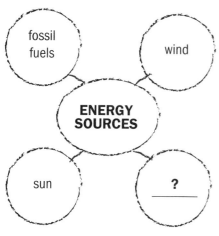

A. waste   **C.** hybrid cars
B. pollution   **D.** nuclear power

2. Find the missing word.

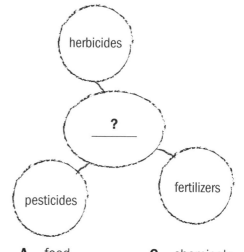

A. food   **C.** chemicals
B. waste   **D.** technologies

DIRECTIONS
Choose the word that best completes each sentence. Circle the letter for the correct answer.

3. Scientists are developing _____ that make cars safer and cleaner.
    A. waste   **C.** chemicals
    B. pollution   **D.** technologies

4. We have to be careful, or we will use up all of Earth's natural _____.
    A. pollution   **C.** technologies
    B. resources   **D.** nuclear power

5. When rain washes chemicals into rivers, it causes water _____.
    A. pollution   **C.** chemicals
    B. resources   **D.** technologies

6. Many traditional buildings _____ energy, so engineers are designing new buildings that save energy.
    A. find   **C.** waste
    B. save   **D.** create

READING: "Changing Earth"

DIRECTIONS
Choose the best answer for each item. Circle the letter for the correct answer.

7. "Changing Earth" is—
   A. a biography.
   B. an interview.
   C. historical fiction.
   D. an informational text.

8. What happened to the human population after 1800?
   A. It grew very fast.
   B. It grew very slowly.
   C. It got smaller each year.
   D. It stayed about the same.

9. Why are scientists trying to increase the food supply?
   A. They want people to stop eating meat.
   B. They think people should eat more food.
   C. There are more people living on Earth now.
   D. Many people want to eat different kinds of foods.

10. Why do some farmers use chemicals on their crops?
   A. To grow bigger, stronger crops
   B. To insert genes from other organisms into their crops
   C. To stop the pollution of rivers and lakes near their crops
   D. To kill all the insects and animals that live near their crops

11. How are electric cars, solar-powered cars, and cars with fuel cells alike?
   A. They burn fossil fuels.
   B. They use nuclear power.
   C. They use clean sources of energy.
   D. They go faster than cars that use gasoline.

12. What is one problem with nuclear power?
   A. It causes air pollution.
   B. It creates radioactive leftover material.
   C. It varies with the time of day and the weather.
   D. It doesn't work as well as other sources of energy.

GO ON

Unit 4 Part 1 Test/Reading: "Changing Earth"

READING: "The Intersection"

DIRECTIONS
Choose the best answer for each item. Circle the letter for the correct answer.

13. The writer of the first letter thinks that horseless carriages will—
- **A.** be fun to drive.
- **B.** cause more traffic problems.
- **C.** solve some of the traffic problems.
- **D.** be quieter than carriages pulled by horses.

14. Which event in 1929 helped solve some of the intersection's traffic problems?
- **A.** A traffic light went up.
- **B.** Houses were pulled down.
- **C.** Motor cars were invented.
- **D.** More people moved to the city.

15. How are the three letters alike?
- **A.** They were written in the same year.
- **B.** They were written by the same person.
- **C.** They describe traffic problems at the same intersection.
- **D.** They explain how new inventions help solve traffic problems.

16. Why did the writers write these letters?
- **A.** To see their names in a newspaper
- **B.** To persuade people to buy new cars
- **C.** To persuade the city to pave the road
- **D.** To persuade people to drive more slowly

GRAMMAR AND WRITING

DIRECTIONS
Read each sentence. Choose the word or words that best complete each sentence. Circle the letter for the correct answer.

17. If the population keeps growing, we _____ more food.
  A. need
  B. needed
  C. will need
  D. will needing

18. It will save energy if people _____ bikes.
  A. ride
  B. rides
  C. riding
  D. will ride

19. If people drive more slowly, we _____ fewer traffic problems.
  A. has
  B. have
  C. will have
  D. will having

20. Chemicals harm the environment if a farmer _____ them incorrectly.
  A. use
  B. uses
  C. will use
  D. will using

DIRECTIONS
Find the sentence that has no mistakes. Circle the letter for the correct sentence.

21. **A.** If we are not careful, we will use up all of Earth's resources.
  B. If we are not careful we will use up all of Earth's resources.
  C. If, we are not careful we will use up all of Earth's resources.
  D. If we are not careful we will use up, all of Earth's resources.

22. **A.** Fish will die, if chemicals get into the rivers.
  B. Fish will die if, chemicals get into the rivers.
  C. Fish will die if chemicals, get into the rivers.
  D. Fish will die if chemicals get into the rivers.

UNIT 4 Part 2 Test

VOCABULARY

DIRECTIONS
Look at the word webs. Find the missing word. Circle the letter for the correct answer.

1. Find the missing word.

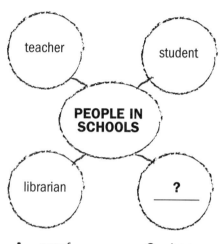

A. proof	**C.** honor
B. trend	**D.** principal

2. Find the missing word.

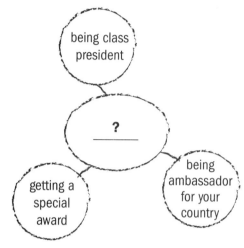

A. trends	**C.** honors
B. proofs	**D.** principals

DIRECTIONS
Choose the word that best completes each sentence. Circle the letter for the correct answer.

3. People who are nice toward others get a _____ for being friendly.
- **A.** trend
- **B.** worthy
- **C.** problem
- **D.** reputation

4. Shirley tried to feel _____ of having such an important job.
- **A.** worthy
- **B.** nervous
- **C.** unhappy
- **D.** surprised

5. Shirley named each year aloud as _____ that she was ten years old.
- **A.** trend
- **B.** proof
- **C.** honor
- **D.** reputation

6. Hanging colorful things on backpacks is a popular _____ for students at my school this year.
- **A.** trend
- **B.** proof
- **C.** principal
- **D.** reputation

GO ON

READING: "China's Little Ambassador"

DIRECTIONS
Choose the best answer for each item. Circle the letter for the correct answer.

7. "China's Little Ambassador" is a chapter from—
   A. a play.
   B. a novel.
   C. an interview.
   D. an autobiography.

8. What is "China's Little Ambassador" mostly about?
   A. What it is like to be an ambassador
   B. Shirley's feelings about her mother
   C. Shirley's new teacher and principal
   D. Shirley's first day at an American school

9. Why does Shirley keep shutting and opening both eyes?
   A. She has a problem with her eyes.
   B. She does not want to cry in front of the other students.
   C. Chinese people shut and open their eyes to show friendship.
   D. She thinks Americans shut and open their eyes to show friendship.

10. Which sentence from the passage is an example of dialogue?
    A. Shirley put up ten fingers.
    B. The class stood up and waved.
    C. Suddenly, Mother hissed in Chinese, "Stop that or else!"
    D. Alone, the headmistress and Shirley looked at each other.

11. Which sentence from the passage is an example of a simile?
    A. The woman had no eyelashes.
    B. Three girls even wore earrings.
    C. One boy was as big as a water jar.
    D. So she shut and opened both eyes.

12. When you use your experience to understand Shirley, you—
    A. ask yourself how you are like Shirley.
    B. skim for details about Shirley.
    C. compare Shirley and the American students.
    D. preview the passage's title, pictures, and a few sentences.

Unit 4 Part 2 Test/Reading: "China's Little Ambassador"

READING: "Migration Patterns"

DIRECTIONS
Choose the best answer for each item. Circle the letter for the correct answer.

13. "Migration Patterns" tells about—
   A. how to move from one place to another.
   B. the best places to live in the United States.
   C. migration patterns in different countries around the world.
   D. where people in the United States move and why they move.

14. You can tell from the passage that most Americans move—
   A. short distances.
   B. long distances.
   C. to other countries.
   D. to other states in a country.

15. Which group of people would be the least likely to move?
   A. People who are not married
   B. People who are 25–29 years old
   C. People who rent the place they live in
   D. People whose husbands or wives have died

16. Which statement about future trends is true?
   A. More people will probably move to the South.
   B. More people will probably move to the Northeast.
   C. More people will probably move to the Midwest.
   D. Married people will probably move more often than single or divorced people.

GRAMMAR AND WRITING

DIRECTIONS
Choose the best answer for each question. Circle the letter for the correct answer.

17. Which of these is an independent clause?
   A. The principal laughed.
   B. After Shirley shut and opened both eyes
   C. When Shirley shut and opened both eyes
   D. Because Shirley shut and opened both eyes

18. Which of these is a dependent clause?
   A. Shirley raised her hand.
   B. She went to the blackboard.
   C. Mrs. Rappaport smiled at her.
   D. When Shirley wrote the correct answer

19. Which word is a subordinating conjunction?
   A. eyes
   B. shuts
   C. when
   D. Shirley

20. Which of these is a complex sentence?
   A. While Shirley looked around the classroom
   B. After the class waved at her, Shirley bowed.
   C. Shirley and the principal walked into the classroom.
   D. Mrs. Rappaport asked a question, and Shirley raised her hand.

DIRECTIONS
Find the sentence that has no mistakes. Circle the letter for the correct sentence.

21. A. When Shirley closed her eyes she dreamed of candy and cookies.
   B. When Shirley closed her eyes she dreamed, of candy and cookies.
   C. When Shirley closed her eyes, she dreamed of candy and cookies.
   D. When, Shirley closed her eyes she dreamed of candy and cookies.

22. A. Shirley gave her father the letter before she went to bed.
   B. Shirley gave her father the letter, before she went to bed.
   C. Shirley gave her father the letter before, she went to bed.
   D. Shirley gave her father the letter, before, she went to bed.

Unit 4 Part 2 Test/Grammar and Writing

UNIT 5 Part 1 Test

VOCABULARY

DIRECTIONS

Look at the word webs. Find the missing word or words. Circle the letter for the correct answer.

1. Find the missing word.

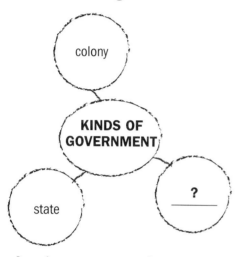

A. siege   **C.** republic
B. conflict   **D.** constitution

2. Find the missing word or words.

A. siege   **C.** constitution
B. republic   **D.** political party

DIRECTIONS

Choose the word that best completes each sentence. Circle the letter for the correct answer.

3. The Americans didn't want to be part of Mexico, which put them in _____ conflict with the Mexican government.
   A. hopeful   **B.** political   **C.** republic   **D.** friendly

4. Santa Anna wanted American settlers to obey Mexican laws, so he sent soldiers to Texas to _____ the laws.
   A. fight   **B.** siege   **C.** enforce   **D.** understand

5. When Texas became a new nation, the people wrote a _____ to describe how the new government would work.
   A. siege   **B.** country   **C.** patriotism   **D.** constitution

6. The Texans showed their _____ by flying the Lone Star flag.
   A. siege   **B.** waving   **C.** airplanes   **D.** patriotism

GO ON

READING: "The Road to Texas Independence"

DIRECTIONS
Choose the best answer for each item. Circle the letter for the correct answer.

7. "The Road to Texas Independence" is—
   A. a diary.
   B. a mystery.
   C. historical fiction.
   D. an informational text.

8. Why did American settlers move to Texas in the early 1800s?
   A. The land in Texas was cheap.
   B. They liked the Mexican government.
   C. They wanted to start their own country.
   D. The U.S. government asked them to leave.

9. American settlers in Texas began to organize armies because they—
   A. wanted to own all of Mexico.
   B. didn't want Texas to be part of Mexico.
   C. were afraid of the *Tejanos* living in Texas.
   D. wanted to get Stephen F. Austin out of prison.

10. What happened at the Alamo?
    A. Texas troops started a siege at the Alamo and won a big battle.
    B. Santa Anna was captured and agreed to make Texas independent.
    C. Mexican soldiers attacked the Alamo and killed many people inside it.
    D. Mexican soldiers surrounded the Alamo, and the Texas troops gave up without a fight.

11. Who was the first president of the Republic of Texas?
    A. Jim Bowie
    B. Sam Houston
    C. General Santa Anna
    D. George Washington

12. When you take notes for "The Road to Texas Independence," you should—
    A. copy each sentence from the text.
    B. write only the names of the people in the text.
    C. make a list of important dates and events in the text.
    D. tell how you would feel if you lived in Texas in the 1800s.

READING: from *A Line in the Sand*

DIRECTIONS

Choose the best answer for each item. Circle the letter for the correct answer.

13. The journal entries from *A Line in the Sand* are—
- **A.** nonfiction.
- **B.** biographies.
- **C.** historical fiction.
- **D.** informational texts.

14. When did the events in these journal entries take place?
- **A.** During the war of 1812
- **B.** Before the war between Texas and Mexico
- **C.** Just after the war between Texas and Mexico
- **D.** After Texas became part of the United States

15. The War Party wanted—
- **A.** Texas to stay part of Mexico.
- **B.** Texas to declare its independence.
- **C.** Mexico to write a new constitution.
- **D.** American settlers to control all of Mexico.

16. You can tell from the passage that Lucinda—
- **A.** often talks as if she knows everything.
- **B.** thinks Texas should not be part of Mexico.
- **C.** thinks farming is too hard and wants to find a new home.
- **D.** loves living in Texas, but worries about having to leave it.

GRAMMAR AND WRITING

DIRECTIONS

Choose the word or words that best complete each sentence. Circle the letter for the correct answer.

17. Mexico's army was _____ Texas's army.
    A. big   **C.** the biggest
    B. bigger than   **D.** more bigger than

18. The battle at the Alamo was one of _____ battles in the war between Mexico and Texas.
    A. the worst   **C.** the baddest
    B. worse than   **D.** the worstest

19. The rider's town was _____ Lucinda's town.
    A. busy   **C.** busier than
    B. the busiest   **D.** more busier than

20. Our farm in Texas is _____ place we have ever seen.
    A. the beautiful   **C.** beautifuller than the
    B. the most beautiful   **D.** more beautiful than the

DIRECTIONS

Find the sentence that has no mistakes. Circle the letter for the correct sentence.

21. **A.** Stephen F. Austin helped many americans move to Texas.
     B. Stephen F. austin helped many Americans move to Texas.
     C. Stephen F. Austin helped many Americans move to texas.
     D. Stephen F. Austin helped many Americans move to Texas.

22. **A.** lucinda Lawrence and her family live on a farm in Gonzales, Texas.
     B. Lucinda Lawrence and her family live on a farm in gonzales, Texas.
     C. Lucinda Lawrence and her family live on a farm in Gonzales, Texas.
     D. Lucinda Lawrence and her Family live on a farm in Gonzales, Texas.

STOP

UNIT 5 Part 2 Test

VOCABULARY

DIRECTIONS
Look at the word webs. Find the missing word. Circle the letter for the correct answer.

1. Find the missing word.

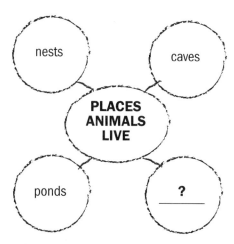

   A. dens
   B. rattles
   C. coyotes
   D. cowboys

2. Find the missing word.

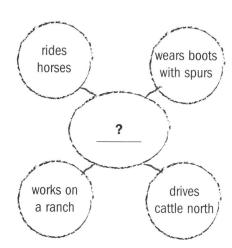

   A. den
   B. pack
   C. wagon
   D. cowboy

DIRECTIONS
Choose the word that best completes each sentence. Circle the letter for the correct answer.

3. Grandy had never met a boy before, so he was _____ and wanted to know more about him.
   A. tired   **C.** curious
   B. bored   **D.** affection

4. Grandy is the leader of the _____ of coyotes.
   A. boy   **C.** promise
   B. pack   **D.** affection

5. By giving Grandy a special name, the coyotes showed _____ for him.
   A. pack   **C.** promise
   B. curious   **D.** affection

6. Grandy wants the animals to _____ that they will not harm the boy.
   A. hurt   **C.** promise
   B. love   **D.** affection

READING: from *Pecos Bill: The Greatest Cowboy of All Time*

DIRECTIONS

Choose the best answer for each item. Circle the letter for the correct answer.

7. The excerpt is—
   A. a tall tale.
   B. a biography.
   C. an interview.
   D. an informational text.

8. Which event in the excerpt happens first?
   A. Grandy teaches Pecos Bill.
   B. Pecos Bill becomes a great cowboy.
   C. Pecos Bill falls out of his family's wagon.
   D. Grandy leads Pecos Bill to the coyotes' dens.

9. When Pecos Bill first meets Grandy, he thinks Grandy is a—
   A. tall cowboy.
   B. friendly dog.
   C. human with long ears.
   D. dangerous wild animal.

10. At the end of the story, how many animals promise not to harm the boy?
   A. All of them
   B. Most of them
   C. Only two animals
   D. None of the animals

11. Which of the following does not describe the Wouser?
   A. He has no friends.
   B. He is big and strong.
   C. He makes his rattle hiss when he is angry.
   D. He is part Mountain Lion and part Grizzly Bear.

12. Which group of words from the passage is an example of hyperbole?
   A. Dug up roots that were sweet and spicy
   B. Running his hands through the long shaggy hair
   C. Crossed the river and disappeared into the sagebush
   D. The healthiest, strongest, most active boy in the world

READING: "The Cowboy Era"

DIRECTIONS

Choose the best answer for each item. Circle the letter for the correct answer.

13. "The Cowboy Era" is a—
   A. poem.
   B. tall tale.
   C. fictional story.
   D. social studies article.

14. Why did Texas ranchers want cowboys to move the cattle north?
   A. No one in Texas wanted to buy the cattle.
   B. They wanted the cattle to get off their land.
   C. They could sell the cattle for more money in other places.
   D. They wanted to start large cattle ranches in the Northeast.

15. The great cattle drives happened—
   A. a few years ago.
   B. after the Civil War ended.
   C. just before the Civil War started.
   D. just after barbed wire was invented.

16. What is one reason the cattle drives ended?
   A. Many cowboys got other jobs.
   B. There were too many stampedes.
   C. Barbed wire closed in the ranges.
   D. Ranchers could not sell the cattle for much money.

GRAMMAR AND WRITING

DIRECTIONS

Choose the word that best completes each sentence. Circle the letter for the correct answer.

17. The cowboy put _____ saddle on the horse.
    A. his   **C.** mine
    B. ours   **D.** theirs

18. I wear boots on _____ feet.
    A. my   **C.** mine
    B. ours   **D.** theirs

19. This horse is yours, and that horse is _____.
    A. my   **C.** mine
    B. her   **D.** their

20. Their ranch is near the river. _____ is near the mountains.
    A. My   **C.** Her
    B. Our   **D.** Ours

DIRECTIONS

Find the sentence that has no mistakes. Circle the letter for the correct sentence.

21. **A.** Tom has a horse, and its name is Dusty.
    B. Tom has a horse, and it's name is Dusty.
    C. Tom has a horse, and i'ts name is Dusty.
    D. Tom has a horse, and its' name is Dusty.

22. **A.** Pecos Bill had red hair short.
    B. Pecos Bill had hair short, red.
    C. Pecos Bill had short, red hair.
    D. Pecos Bill short, red hair he had.

UNIT 6 Part 1 Test

VOCABULARY

DIRECTIONS
Look at the word webs. Find the missing words. Circle the letter for the correct answer.

1. Find the missing words.

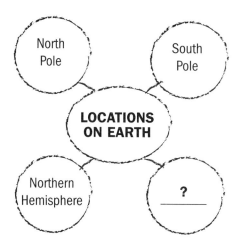

    A. Roman calendar
    B. ancient Egyptians
    C. spring equinox
    D. Southern Hemisphere

2. Find the missing words.

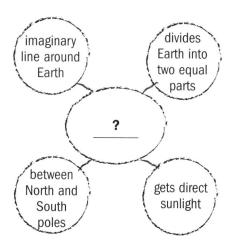

    A. the equator
    B. Earth's axis
    C. Earth's orbit
    D. Earth's poles

DIRECTIONS
Choose the word that best completes each sentence. Circle the letter for the correct answer.

3. Earth turns on its _____.
    A. axis   **C.** equator
    B. orbit   **D.** North Pole

4. It takes Earth 24 hours to complete one _____, or turn.
    A. axis   **C.** equator
    B. orbit   **D.** rotation

5. Earth moves in an oval _____ around the sun.
    A. axis   **C.** equator
    B. orbit   **D.** rotation

6. It is usually hot at the _____.
    A. axis   **C.** equator
    B. orbit   **D.** rotation

READING: "Earth's Orbit"

DIRECTIONS
Choose the best answer for each item. Circle the letter for the correct answer.

7. "Earth's Orbit" is—
  A. a myth.
  B. nonfiction.
  C. science fiction.
  D historical fiction.

8. What causes day and night?
  A. The seasons
  B. The equator
  C. The North and South poles
  D. Earth's rotation on its axis

9. Earth's orbit around the sun takes about—
  A. 24 hours.
  B. 29 days.
  C. 365 days.
  D. 4 years.

10. Look at the diagram below. What does the arrow show? Circle the letter for the correct answer.
  A. Earth's axis
  B. Earth's orbit
  C. Earth's rotation
  D. The sun's movement

11. What happens when the northern part of Earth is tilted toward the sun?
  A. Earth's orbit speeds up.
  B. The equator gets colder.
  C. It is summer in the Northern Hemisphere.
  D. It is summer in the Southern Hemisphere.

12. The shortest day of the year in the Northern Hemisphere is the—
  A. winter solstice.
  B. spring equinox.
  C. summer solstice.
  D. autumnal equinox.

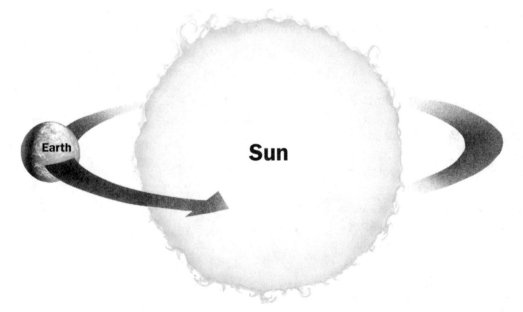

Earth revolves around the sun.

Name _____   Date _____

READING: "How Glooskap Found the Summer" and "Persephone and the Pomegranate Seeds"

DIRECTIONS
Choose the best answer for each item. Circle the letter for the correct answer.

"How Glooskap Found the Summer"

13. What problem did the Wawaniki people have?
    A. It was too cold for food to grow.
    B. It was too hot, and all the plants died.
    C. They didn't have a strong leader to help them.
    D. Summer spent six months in their country each year.

14. Who is the hero of "How Glooskap Found the Summer"?
    A. Winter
    B. Glooskap
    C. Tattler the Loon
    D. the Wawaniki people

"Persephone and the Pomegranate Seeds"

15. The main conflict in "Persephone and the Pomegranate Seeds" is between—
    A. Zeus and Hermes.
    B. Pluto and Demeter.
    C. Persephone and Hermes.
    D. Persephone and Demeter.

16. What is one way that "How Glooskap Found the Summer" and "Persephone and the Pomegranate Seeds" are alike?
    A. Both texts have characters who are seasons.
    B. The texts are old stories told by the same culture.
    C. Both texts have events that take place under Earth.
    D. Both texts are myths that explain why Earth has seasons.

GRAMMAR AND WRITING

DIRECTIONS

Find the sentence that has no mistakes. Circle the letter for the correct sentence.

17. **A.** I must save my people, "Glooskap thought."
    B. I must save my people, Glooskap thought.
    C. "I must save my people, Glooskap thought."
    D. "I must save my people," Glooskap thought.

18. **A.** Then Summer said. "I have proved that I am stronger than you,"
    B. Then Summer "said, I have proved that I am stronger than you."
    C. Then Summer said, "I have proved that I am stronger than you."
    D. Then Summer said, "I have proved that I am stronger than you?"

19. **A.** "I will accept your offer," Winter whispered sadly.
    B. "I will accept your offer." Winter whispered sadly.
    C. "I will accept your offer, Winter whispered sadly.
    D. "I will accept your offer, Winter whispered sadly."

20. **A.** "Persephone, did you eat the twelve seeds," he inquired?
    B. "Persephone, did you eat the twelve seeds?" he inquired.
    C. "Persephone, did you eat the twelve seeds," he inquired.
    D. Persephone, "did you eat the twelve seeds?" he inquired.

DIRECTIONS

Find the sentence that uses the correct reporting verb. Circle the letter for the correct sentence.

21. **A.** "My power is gone!" Winter cried.
    B. "My power is gone!" Winter asked.
    C. "My power is gone!" Winter thought.
    D. "My power is gone!" Winter murmured.

22. **A.** "Do you know where the queen lives?" Glooskap said.
    B. "Do you know where the queen lives?" Glooskap asked.
    C. "Do you know where the queen lives?" Glooskap replied.
    D. "Do you know where the queen lives?" Glooskap thought.

Name _____ Date _____

UNIT 6 Part 2 Test

VOCABULARY

DIRECTIONS
Look at the word webs. Find the missing word. Circle the letter for the correct answer.

1. Find the missing word.

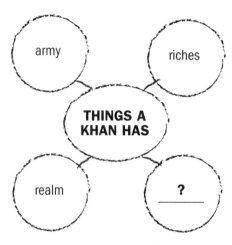

A. poor	**C.** palace
B. stars	**D.** narrator

2. Find the missing word.

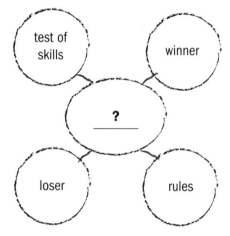

A. palace	**C.** conquer
B. contest	**D.** adventurer

DIRECTIONS
Choose the word or words that best complete each sentence. Circle the letter for the correct answer.

3. People who enjoy facing challenges and doing exciting things are _____.
   A. palaces   **C.** contests
   B. mountains   **D.** adventurers

4. The khan wants his army to _____ his enemies, so he can have his enemies' land.
   A. enter   **C.** travel
   B. meet   **D.** conquer

5. If the khan gets more land, his _____ will get bigger.
   A. play   **C.** conquer
   B. realm   **D.** adventurer

6. Mountain Lifter was stronger than Chief Wrestler, so he won the wrestling _____.
   A. match   **C.** palace
   B. realm   **D.** adventurer

READING: *The Great Bear*

DIRECTIONS

Choose the best answer for each item. Circle the letter for the correct answer.

7. Who introduces the two hunters and explains other parts of the play?
   A. the khan
   B. the narrator
   C. the khan's son
   D. the adventurers

8. Which of these is a stage direction?
   A. **SCENE 1**
   B. **SKY SHOOTER:**
   C. *(SKY SHOOTER enters, gazing up at the sky.)*
   D. This morning I shot a bird flying in the heaven and now I'm waiting for it to fall.

9. Why do the adventurers go to the khan's palace?
   A. To serve the khan
   B. To win the khan's contests
   C. To ask the khan to solve a problem for them
   D. To stop the khan from conquering their empire

10. How are the adventurers alike?
   A. All are very strong.
   B. All can hear very well.
   C. All have a special skill.
   D. All are afraid of the khan.

11. What happens to the adventurers at the end of the play?
   A. They become stars in a constellation.
   B. They are killed in a fire inside the palace.
   C. They look for adventures in a new country.
   D. They become the new rulers in the khan's realm.

12. Before your class reads a play aloud, the first thing you should do is—
   A. listen carefully to other actors so you know when to say your lines.
   B. read the list of characters and decide who will read each character's lines.
   C. use the stage directions to help you read your lines and move on the stage.
   D. read the play to yourself and study your character's lines and the stage directions.

READING: "Telescopes"

DIRECTIONS
Choose the best answer for each item. Circle the letter for the correct answer.

13. Astronomers use light rays to help them—
   A. make telescopes smaller.
   B. make images look bigger.
   C. make telescopes less expensive.
   D. get information about the planets and stars.

14. A refracting telescope is—
   A. very large.
   B. very simple.
   C. made with mirrors.
   D. often put on a mountaintop.

15. Which of these does <u>not</u> describe a reflecting telescope?
   A. It has no lens.
   B. It has an eyepiece lens.
   C. Light bounces off a mirror inside it.
   D. It is often used by professional astronomers.

16. What happens if you look at bright lights before you go outside to watch stars?
   A. It will take you longer to get full night vision.
   B. It will take you less time to get full night vision.
   C. The eyepiece lens on your telescope won't work as well.
   D. You won't be able to see anything outside for many hours.

GRAMMAR AND WRITING

DIRECTIONS

Choose the word that best completes each sentence. Circle the letter for the correct answer.

17. *The Great Bear* is a play _____ seven adventurers.
   A. at   **C.** under
   B. in   **D.** about

18. The hunters were walking _____ the Ordos Desert.
   A. of   **C.** with
   B. in   **D.** under

19. The hunters met a young man _____ a bow and arrows.
   A. at   **C.** with
   B. on   **D.** about

20. The school play starts _____ 7:00.
   A. at   **C.** of
   B. in   **D.** with

DIRECTIONS

Choose the best answer for each question. Circle the letter for the correct answer.

21. Which group of words shows the correct way to write dialogue for a play?
   A. **swift runner:** LET'S GO HOME!
   B. **SWIFT RUNNER** Let's go home!
   C. **SWIFT RUNNER:** Let's go home!
   D. **SWIFT RUNNER:** "Let's go home!"

22. Which group of words shows the correct way to write stage directions for a play?
   A. *(Great Listener puts her ear to the ground.*
   B. *GREAT LISTENER puts her ear to the ground.*
   C. *(GREAT LISTENER puts her ear to the ground.)*
   D. *(GREAT LISTENER PUTS HER EAR TO THE GROUND.)*

STOP

Shining Star B

Unit Tests

UNIT 1 Test

LISTENING Passage: "The Land Bridge to North America"

DIRECTIONS

Listen to the passage. Then choose the best answer for each item. Circle the letter for the correct answer.

1. Which two places did the land bridge join?
   - **A.** North America and Siberia
   - **B.** Siberia and South America
   - **C.** North America and South America
   - **D.** Central America and South America

2. Why did hunters cross the land bridge?
   - **A.** The ice began to melt.
   - **B.** They probably followed the animals.
   - **C.** They wanted to get to South America.
   - **D.** They wanted to get away from the animals.

3. How did the land bridge get under water?
   - **A.** It rained for years.
   - **B.** There was a big storm.
   - **C.** The ice began to melt.
   - **D.** Too many people used the bridge.

4. Over time, some of the people in North America—
   - **A.** moved north.
   - **B.** moved south.
   - **C.** swam back across the water.
   - **D.** sailed a boat back across the water.

GO ON

Name _____   Date _____

PHONICS AND SPELLING

DIRECTIONS
Choose the word with the same sound as the underlined part of the word in the box. Circle the letter for the correct answer.

5. came
   A. fall
   B. rain
   C. land
   D. farmer

6. teeth
   A. them
   B. herd
   C. they
   D. meat

7. hill
   A. fish
   B. ride
   C. bird
   D. train

8. wife
   A. dirt
   B. pain
   C. night
   D. built

9. red
   A. eat
   B. tree
   C. game
   D. ahead

DIRECTIONS
Choose the word that is spelled correctly and completes the sentence. Circle the letter for the correct answer.

10. The Northeast _____ great forests.
   A. had
   B. hed
   C. hade
   D. head

11. They carved an _____ on the totem pole.
   A. igle
   B. egle
   C. eegle
   D. eagle

12. Many people died on the _____ of Tears.
   A. Trayl
   B. Trail
   C. Trial
   D. Trael

13. Sacagawea was away from her family for a long _____.
   A. tim
   B. tyme
   C. time
   D. tame

14. We _____ take a test about the readings next week.
   A. will
   B. well
   C. wall
   D. wyll

VOCABULARY

DIRECTIONS
Choose the best answer for each item. Circle the letter for the correct answer.

15. <u>Nomads</u> are people who—
   A. live in one place for a long time.
   B. translate languages for others.
   C. move from one place to another place.
   D. study objects and peoples from long ago.

16. If you don't speak someone's language, you need—
   A. a nomad.
   B. an interpreter.
   C. an expedition.
   D. an environment.

17. What is another word for <u>expedition</u>?
   A. farm
   B. home
   C. canoe
   D. journey

18. Which word means the same as <u>dry</u>?
   A. arid
   B. region
   C. climate
   D. irrigate

DIRECTIONS
Choose the word that best completes each sentence. Circle the letter for the correct answer.

19. The Southeast has a mild _____ that is not too hot or too cold.
   A. arid
   B. tribe
   C. climate
   D. interpreter

20. The Cherokee were forced to leave the Southeast _____.
   A. tribe
   B. region
   C. nomad
   D. moccasin

21. Native Americans wore _____ on their feet.
   A. tribes
   B. regions
   C. nomads
   D. moccasins

22. Sacagawea had to live with the Minnetaree after they _____ her.
   A. trade
   B. irrigate
   C. kidnapped
   D. recognized

GO ON ▶

READING: "The First Americans"

DIRECTIONS
Choose the best answer for each item.

23. How do some scientists think the first Americans got to North America?
    A. White settlers forced them to move to North America.
    B. They flew planes across the ocean to North America.
    C. They crossed a land bridge from Siberia to North America.
    D. They walked north from South America to North America.

24. Which of the following describes the Northeast region?
    A. It is hot and arid.
    B. It has a mild climate.
    C. It has mostly flat, grassy lands.
    D. It has many forests, rivers, and lakes.

25. Why were buffalo important to the Plains tribes?
    A. They used them for food and to make things.
    B. They raised them and sold them to the Spanish.
    C. They rode them when they hunted other animals.
    D. They used them to help them plant crops in fields.

26. Many Northwest tribes made family trees by carving animals in—
    A. books.
    B. buffalo.
    C. potlatches.
    D. totem poles.

27. After you preview a passage, you make a prediction about—
    A. who wrote the passage.
    B. what the passage is about.
    C. why the author wrote the passage.
    D. what you already know about the subject.

28. You can tell that "The First Americans" is nonfiction because it tells about—
    A. Native American tribes.
    B. real people and places.
    C. imaginary people and places.
    D. events that will happen in the future.

GO ON ▶

Unit 1 Test/Reading: "The First Americans"

READING: "This Land Is Your Land" and "Roll On, Columbia"

DIRECTIONS

Choose the best answer for each item. Circle the letter for the correct answer.

"This Land Is Your Land"

29. "This Land Is Your Land" describes—
    A. only places in California.
    B. only places in New York.
    C. places in the United States.
    D. people in the United States.

30. When a poet uses alliteration such as "roamed and rambled," some of the words have—
    A. the same meaning.
    B. the same ending sounds.
    C. the same middle sounds.
    D. the same beginning sounds.

"Roll On, Columbia"

31. In this passage, the words *roll on* describe—
    A. where the Columbia River is.
    B. how the Columbia River moves.
    C. what the Columbia River looks like.
    D. things you can see in the Columbia River.

32. You can tell that Woody Guthrie considered the Columbia River—
    A. not interesting.
    B. not useful.
    C. strong and powerful.
    D. scary and dangerous.

Name _____   Date _____

READING: from *River to Tomorrow*

DIRECTIONS

Choose the best answer for each item. Circle the letter for the correct answer.

33. *River to Tomorrow* is—
- **A.** a song.
- **B.** a poem.
- **C.** nonfiction.
- **D.** historical fiction.

34. Why did Sacagawea leave her Shoshone village?
- **A.** The Minnetaree took her away.
- **B.** She wanted to live with the Minnetaree.
- **C.** She wanted to help Lewis and Clark.
- **D.** She wanted to travel to new places.

35. Which event from the passage is an example of a flashback?
- **A.** Captain Clark drew a map on the ground.
- **B.** Sacagawea thought about tomorrow.
- **C.** Sacagawea hugged her brother as tears ran down her face.
- **D.** Sacagawea remembered what happened to her village five years ago.

36. The passage says the explorers planned to go to "the Shining Mountains where the snow never melted." You can tell from these words that the Shining Mountains were—
- **A.** not very big.
- **B.** dark and ugly.
- **C.** high and cold.
- **D.** covered with trees.

37. How did Sacagawea feel when she recognized her brother?
- **A.** Happy
- **B.** Scared
- **C.** Angry
- **D.** Lonely

38. What is another good title for the passage?
- **A.** "Sacagawea Gets Kidnapped"
- **B.** "Sacagawea Finds Her People"
- **C.** "Traveling on a River to the Northwest"
- **D.** "The Shoshone and the Minnetaree Tribes"

Unit 1 Test/Reading: from *River to Tomorrow*

Name _____ Date _____

READING: "Reading a Relief Map"

DIRECTIONS
Choose the best answer for each item. Circle the letter for the correct answer.

39. "Reading a Relief Map" is—
   A. fiction.
   B. historical fiction.
   C. a newspaper article.
   D. an informational text.

40. When you read a relief map, you can find out—
   A. how many people live in a region.
   B. what kind of climate the region has.
   C. interesting places to visit in a region.
   D. the location of plains, hills, or mountains in a region.

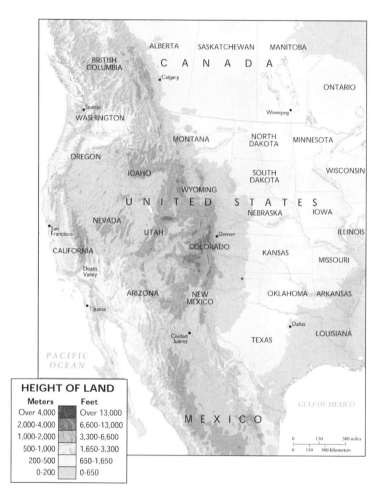

41. Look at the relief map above. Which region has the lowest elevation?
   A. Plains
   B. Southeast
   C. Southwest
   D. Northwest

42. Most mountains are probably—
   A. at sea level.
   B. below sea level.
   C. above sea level.
   D. the same elevation as plains.

GRAMMAR

DIRECTIONS
Read each pair of sentences. Look at the underlined word in the first sentence. Then choose the correct pronoun to complete the second sentence. Circle the letter for the correct answer.

43. The redwood <u>forest</u> is in the Northwest. _____ is full of huge trees.
    A. It   **C.** They
    B. We   **D.** Them

44. The Plains people had <u>horses</u>. The men used _____ to hunt buffalo.
    A. it   **C.** they
    B. him   **D.** them

45. <u>My parents and I</u> are Navaho. _____ live in Arizona.
    A. He   **C.** Us
    B. We   **D.** You

DIRECTIONS
Choose the conjunction that best completes the sentence. Circle the letter for the correct answer.

46. Sacagawea held the moccasin _____ looked at it carefully.
    A. or   **C.** but
    B. and   **D.** with

47. On some days, Sacagawea either rode in the boat _____ walked along the shore.
    A. or   **C.** but
    B. so   **D.** and

DIRECTIONS
Find the sentence that has no mistakes. Circle the letter for the correct sentence.

48. **A.** Some Northwest tribes lived near the ocean, and it hunted whales.
    B. Some Northwest tribes lived near the ocean, and we hunted whales.
    C. Some Northwest tribes lived near the ocean, and they hunted whales.
    D. Some Northwest tribes lived near the ocean, and them hunted whales.

49. **A.** Sacagawea didn't see her brother or her village for five years.
    B. Sacagawea didn't see her brother not her village for five years.
    C. Sacagawea didn't see her brother with her village for five years.
    D. Sacagawea didn't see her brother but her village for five years.

50. **A.** When Sacagawea saw her brother, she shouted his name or cried.
    B. When Sacagawea saw her brother, she shouted his name but cried.
    C. When Sacagawea saw her brother, she shouted his name for cried.
    D. When Sacagawea saw her brother, she shouted his name and cried.

WRITING

WRITING PROMPT

Think of an interesting place. It can be a real or imaginary place. It can be beautiful or scary.

Write a description of this place. Tell what you can see and do there. Tell how it feels to be there. Be sure to include details that help readers picture the place. Write on the lines below.

STOP

UNIT 2 Test

LISTENING Passage: "Making My First Campfire"

DIRECTIONS

Listen to the passage. Then choose the best answer for each item. Circle the letter for the correct answer.

1. What does the narrator do in this passage?
   A. Puts up a tent
   B. Makes a campfire
   C. Cooks food on a campfire
   D. Tells Dad how to make a campfire

2. What is the first thing to do when you make a campfire?
   A. Dig a pit in the ground.
   B. Use a match to light the tinder.
   C. Add more hardwood to the fire.
   D. Put softwood into the shape of a tepee.

3. What should you do after the fire starts?
   A. Dig a pit in the ground.
   B. Add more firewood to the fire.
   C. Add more tinder to the fire.
   D. Put kindling into the shape of a tepee.

4. How does the narrator feel at the end of the passage?
   A. Sad
   B. Tired
   C. Angry
   D. Excited

PHONICS AND SPELLING

DIRECTIONS
Choose the word with the same sound as the underlined part of the word in the box. Circle the letter for the correct answer.

5. | r<u>o</u>ck |
   - A. you
   - B. job
   - C. roll
   - D. coat

6. | t<u>oa</u>ds |
   - A. top
   - B. tall
   - C. hole
   - D. food

7. | b<u>u</u>gs |
   - A. sun
   - B. you
   - C. cute
   - D. loud

8. | m<u>u</u>les |
   - A. sun
   - B. hunts
   - C. mouse
   - D. human

9. | h<u>i</u>ke |
   - A. him
   - B. sick
   - C. knee
   - D. mile

DIRECTIONS
Choose the word that is spelled correctly and completes the sentence. Circle the letter for the correct answer.

10. It is _____ to play outside.
    - A. fon
    - B. fun
    - C. fan
    - D. fin

11. The bird has a nest in the _____ of the tree.
    - A. top
    - B. tup
    - C. tope
    - D. toop

12. The plants _____ tall after it rained.
    - A. groo
    - B. grue
    - C. grew
    - D. grou

13. The fish _____ out of the water.
    - A. jumpt
    - B. jumped
    - C. jumpped
    - D. jumpeed

14. Sam _____ to start a fire.
    - A. tried
    - B. tryed
    - C. tryied
    - D. triyed

VOCABULARY

DIRECTIONS
Choose the best answer for each question. Circle the letter for the correct answer.

15. What kind of animal eats only other animals?
  A. A bark
  B. A herbivore
  C. A carnivore
  D. An omnivore

16. What is the land on the side of a river called?
  A. A line
  B. A bank
  C. A grub
  D. An organism

17. What are animals that you trap or hunt called?
  A. line
  B. bark
  C. grub
  D. game

18. What kind of animal eats only plants?
  A. A bank
  B. A carnivore
  C. A herbivore
  D. An omnivore

DIRECTIONS
Choose the word that best completes each sentence. Circle the letter for the correct answer.

19. A snake and a spider _____ when they use the same rock for shelter.
  A. die
  B. grow
  C. interact
  D. reproduce

20. Water, soil, plants, and animals can all be part of the same _____.
  A. organism
  B. omnivore
  C. carnivore
  D. ecosystem

21. Sam used _____ from a tree to make a fishhook.
  A. bark
  B. bank
  C. grub
  D. game

22. Sam put the hook in the water, and he soon got a _____ from a fish.
  A. bite
  B. line
  C. bark
  D. game

READING: "Ecosystems: The Systems of Nature"

DIRECTIONS
Choose the best answer for each item.

23. The place where an organism lives is called—
   A. a forest.
   B. a habitat.
   C. an offspring.
   D. a carnivore.

24. Which of these is <u>not</u> a living thing?
   A. A mouse
   B. A person
   C. A tree
   D. Sunlight

25. An ecosystem is made up of—
   A. only nonliving things.
   B. only plants and animals.
   C. living and nonliving things in the same area.
   D. all the living and nonliving things in the world.

26. What eats the medium-size fish in an ocean food chain?
   A. Big fish
   B. Small fish
   C. Plants
   D. Water

27. When you skim a passage, you should read—
   A. very quickly.
   B. slowly and carefully.
   C. each sentence in the passage.
   D. only the title and the headings.

28. An informational text—
   A. is fiction.
   B. has rhythm and rhyme.
   C. is nonfiction.
   D. has imaginary characters.

READING: "The Bat" and "The Snake"

DIRECTIONS

Choose the best answer for each item. Circle the letter for the correct answer.

"The Bat"

29. Which words from the poem help you picture what a bat looks like?
- **A.** The attic of an aging house
- **B.** Trees that face the corner light
- **C.** Something is amiss or out of place
- **D.** Mice with wings can wear a human face

30. When two words rhyme, they—
- **A.** have the same ending sounds.
- **B.** have the same number of letters.
- **C.** have the same beginning sounds.
- **D.** tell how an animal is like a person.

"The Snake"

31. "The Snake" is—
- **A.** a song.
- **B.** a poem.
- **C.** a science text.
- **D.** an informational text.

32. Which words does the author use to describe a snake?
- **A.** A narrow fellow
- **B.** Too cool for corn
- **C.** A tighter breathing
- **D.** Zero at the bone

READING: from *My Side of the Mountain*

DIRECTIONS
Choose the best answer for each item. Circle the letter for the correct answer.

33. The events in the passage take place—
   A. in a forest.
   B. in a desert.
   C. in a cave.
   D. near the ocean.

34. What is the first thing Sam does in the passage?
   A. He makes a bed.
   B. He catches a fish.
   C. He makes a fishhook.
   D. He tries to make a fire.

35. What problem does Sam have at the end of the passage?
   A. He can't find any firewood.
   B. He can't get a fire started.
   C. His bed won't stay together.
   D. Animals come into his tent.

36. The passage says that Sam's fishing line "came to life, and rode back and forth and around in a circle." These words are an example of—
   A. rhyme.
   B. flashback.
   C. alliteration.
   D. personification.

37. How can you tell that Sam enjoys making things?
   A. Sam says that he has always been good at whittling.
   B. He finds a good place to fish.
   C. He likes to read.
   D. Another character in the passage says that Sam likes to make things.

38. When you identify with Sam, you—
   A. pay attention to the pictures.
   B. make up your own fictional story about Sam.
   C. compare Sam with other characters from other passages.
   D. ask yourself whether you would feel and act the same way as Sam.

GO ON

READING: "Water and Living Things"

DIRECTIONS
Choose the best answer for each item. Circle the letter for the correct answer.

39. Most of Earth's water is—
   A. salt water.
   B. fresh water.
   C. groundwater.
   D. water vapor.

40. What is the water cycle?
   A. How rain comes from clouds in the sky
   B. How people and animals use Earth's water
   C. What people should do to keep water clean
   D. How Earth's water moves from one place to another

41. What makes water evaporate?
   A. Rain
   B. Clouds
   C. The sun's heat
   D. Salt in the ocean's water

42. What happens when the water drops in clouds get heavy?
   A. They change into a very light gas.
   B. They change into smaller water drops.
   C. They rise in the air and form more clouds.
   D. They fall to Earth as rain, snow, sleet, or hail.

GRAMMAR

DIRECTIONS
Choose the word that best completes each sentence. Circle the letter for the correct answer.

43. A bear _____ in a cave during the winter.
  A. sleep   **C.** sleepy
  B. sleeps   **D.** sleeping

44. Mushrooms _____ along the riverbank.
  A. grow   **C.** grown
  B. grows   **D.** growing

45. Sam sits _____ by the stream.
  A. quiet   **C.** quietly
  B. quieter   **D.** quietest

46. The sky _____ got dark.
  A. quick   **C.** quicker
  B. quickly   **D.** quickest

47. I _____ use worms when I fish.
  A. off   **C.** oftenly
  B. often   **D.** oftenest

DIRECTIONS
Find the sentence that has no mistakes. Circle the letter for the correct sentence.

48. **A.** The bat eat the insect.
    B. The bat eats the insect.
    C. The bats eats the insects.
    D. The bats eating the insects.

49. **A.** My brother and I watch the deer in the field.
    B. My brother and I watches the deer in the field.
    C. My brothers and I watches the deer in the field.
    D. My brothers and I watching the deer in the field.

50. **A.** The fish swam rapid in the stream.
    B. The fish swam rapidly in the stream.
    C. The fish swam rapidier in the stream.
    D. The fish swam rapidest in the stream.

WRITING

WRITING PROMPT

Think of something that you know how to make. For example, you might know how to make a special food or how to make an interesting gift.

Write a paragraph to explain how to make something. Tell what steps you take to make this thing. Put the steps in order. Use sequence words to make the steps easier to follow. Write on the lines below.

_____

_____

_____

_____

_____

_____

_____

_____

_____

_____

_____

_____

_____

_____

_____

_____

_____

_____

_____

UNIT 3 Test

LISTENING Passage: "George Washington Carver, Scientist"

DIRECTIONS

Listen to the passage. Then choose the best answer for each item. Circle the letter for the correct answer.

1. This passage is—
   - **A.** a poem.
   - **B.** a biography.
   - **C.** historical fiction.
   - **D.** an autobiography.

2. What happened when farmers grew cotton crops every year?
   - **A.** It harmed the soil.
   - **B.** It made the soil better.
   - **C.** Farmers grew better crops.
   - **D.** Farmers made more money.

3. How did George Washington Carver help farmers?
   - **A.** He told them to rotate their crops.
   - **B.** He told them to invent new things.
   - **C.** He told them to grow cotton more often.
   - **D.** He told them to stop growing sweet potatoes.

4. What would be another good title for this passage?
   - **A.** "Growing Cotton"
   - **B.** "The Work of a Farmer"
   - **C.** "From Slave to Scientist"
   - **D.** "A History of Slaves in America"

GO ON

PHONICS AND SPELLING

DIRECTIONS

Choose the word with the same sound as the underlined part of the word in the box. Circle the letter for the correct answer.

5. | turn |
    A. her
    B. rule
    C. arm
    D. heart

6. | bird |
    A. braid
    B. hair
    C. rich
    D. nurse

7. | farm |
    A. year
    B. shark
    C. learn
    D. father

8. | wheat |
    A. how
    B. writer
    C. when
    D. wrong

9. | white |
    A. why
    B. wrap
    C. throw
    D. whole

DIRECTIONS

Choose the word that is spelled correctly and completes the sentence. Circle the letter for the correct answer.

10. Frida Kahlo was a famous _____, and her pictures are in museums.
    A. paint
    B. paintar
    C. painter
    D. paintor

11. Christopher Reeve was a horseback _____ before he injured his spinal cord.
    A. ridir
    B. rider
    C. ridur
    D. reyder

12. Dr. Mae Jemison is a famous space _____.
    A. travelor
    B. traveler
    C. travelur
    D. travelour

13. Virgil poured _____ on the lettuce seeds.
    A. water
    B. hwater
    C. wahter
    D. waiter

14. The boy laughed when his father told a _____.
    A. goke
    B. yoke
    C. joke
    D. jhoke

Unit 3 Test/Phonics and Spelling

VOCABULARY

DIRECTIONS

Choose the best answer for each item. Circle the letter for the correct answer.

15. A <u>plantation</u> is a—
  A. crop.
  B. package.
  C. large farm.
  D. large plant.

16. What is an <u>autobiography</u>?
  A. A story about a person's life written by that person
  B. A story about a person's life written by another person
  C. The name that a famous person writes on a piece of paper
  D. A story about an ordinary person written by a famous person

17. Which of these has about the same meaning as <u>distribute</u>?
  A. get
  B. hurt
  C. grow up
  D. give out

18. Something that happens every day is—
  A. strange.
  B. special.
  C. ordinary.
  D. a coincidence.

DIRECTIONS

Choose the word or words that best complete each sentence. Circle the letter for the correct answer.

19. Naomi Shihab Nye writes about people from different cultures who have different ideas and _____.
  A. packages
  B. passengers
  C. coincidences
  D. points of view

20. Dr. Mae Jemison and the six other _____ traveled in space for seven days.
  A. packages
  B. astronauts
  C. plantations
  D. autobiographies

21. Virgil and his dad dug in the _____ with shovels.
  A. seed
  B. ground
  C. package
  D. coincidence

22. The hot sun made the lettuce _____ and die.
  A. wilt
  B. ground
  C. distribute
  D. traditional

GO ON

READING: "Success Stories"

Choose the best answer for each item. Circle the letter for the correct answer.

23. "Success Stories" tells about—
    A. the author's own life story.
    B. real people, places, and events.
    C. imaginary people, places, and events.
    D. imaginary people, but real places and events.

24. Frida Kahlo's self-portraits were pictures of—
    A. herself.
    B. her friends.
    C. her husband.
    D. arranged flowers or fruit.

25. What inference can you make about Naomi Shihab Nye from reading the passage?
    A. She only likes to write poems.
    B. She thinks that all cultures are alike.
    C. She usually writes about famous people.
    D. She enjoys writing about people and places.

26. Tim Berners-Lee invented the—
    A. Internet.
    B. printing press.
    C. first computer.
    D. World Wide Web.

27. Who designed the Vietnam Veterans Memorial?
    A. Maya Lin
    B. Frida Kahlo
    C. Dr. Mae Jemison
    D. Christopher Reeve

28. How are all the people in "Success Stories" alike?
    A. All are artists or actors.
    B. All faced a serious injury or disease.
    C. All have done something difficult.
    D. All are the world's most successful people.

GO ON

READING: "An Interview with Naomi Shihab Nye"

DIRECTIONS
Choose the best answer for each item. Circle the letter for the correct answer.

29. What does an interviewer do?
   A. Writes poems
   B. Asks questions
   C. Answers questions
   D. Watches people on TV

30. In "An Interview with Naomi Shihab Nye," why do the letters <u>RB</u> or <u>NSN</u> appear at the beginning of the paragraphs?
   A. To show you who said the words
   B. To tell you where and when the interview happened
   C. To show you which magazine published the interview
   D. To show you which paragraphs have words that rhyme

31. When Nye first started writing, she wrote about—
   A. animals and trees.
   B. her travels to other places.
   C. her Palestinian grandmother.
   D. things that young writers should do.

32. What is a <u>writing circle</u>?
   A. A special place where you can write
   B. A kind of word web that helps you plan your writing
   C. A group of writers who read and discuss their writing
   D. A traditional dance that Nye does before she starts writing

READING: from *Seedfolks*

DIRECTIONS
Choose the best answer for each item. Circle the letter for the correct answer.

33. The events in the chapter from *Seedfolks* take place during—
   A. the fall.
   B. the winter.
   C. the spring.
   D. the summer.

34. How does Virgil feel when Miss Fleck says the garden looks like a plantation?
   A. Sad
   B. Proud
   C. Angry
   D. Embarrassed

35. What mistake did Virgil's dad make?
   A. He didn't take care of the dirt.
   B. He used the wrong kind of lettuce seeds.
   C. He planted the seeds at the wrong time of year.
   D. He washed the seeds out of place when he watered them.

36. Why was Virgil angry near the end of the story?
   A. He will not get money to buy a new bike.
   B. The girl in the locket refused to save the lettuce.
   C. He didn't have time to ride his bike with his friends.
   D. His dad lied to Miss Fleck about who owned the garden.

37. How can you tell that the chapter from *Seedfolks* uses the first-person point of view?
   A. The author includes dialogue in the chapter.
   B. Virgil is a character who tells about his own life.
   C. The father tells about his own life.
   D. The author writes about characters that are like real people.

38. Which of the following is <u>not</u> a good way to monitor, or check, your comprehension of the chapter from *Seedfolks*?
   A. Reread the passage.
   B. Read the passage quickly.
   C. Put information about the passage in your own words.
   D. Look for answers to questions you have about the passage.

Unit 3 Test/Reading: from *Seedfolks*

READING: "How Seeds and Plants Grow"

DIRECTIONS
Choose the best answer for each item. Circle the letter for the correct answer.

39. "How Seeds and Plants Grow" uses—
   A. only facts.
   B. only opinions.
   C. just a few facts.
   D. a mix of facts and opinions.

40. The time when the embryo first begins to grow is called—
   A. stem.
   B. inactive.
   C. cotyledon.
   D. germination.

41. What happens to the embryo's roots after the seed coat breaks open?
   A. They produce leaves.
   B. They break out of the ground.
   C. They grow down into the ground.
   D. They straighten up toward the sunlight.

42. What happens during photosynthesis?
   A. The plant makes its own food.
   B. The embryo eats its stored food.
   C. The stem breaks out of the ground.
   D. The embryo breaks out of its seed coat.

GO ON

GRAMMAR

DIRECTIONS
Choose the word that best completes each sentence. Circle the letter for the correct answer.

43. _____ Maya Lin design the Vietnam Veterans Memorial?
    A. Why   **C.** Did
    B. How   **D.** Where

44. _____ traveled in space aboard the *Endeavour*?
    A. Who   **C.** When
    B. How   **D.** Where

45. _____ did Christopher Reeve do after his accident?
    A. Why   **C.** When
    B. What   **D.** Where

46. The sun was hot, _____ the lettuce started to wilt and die.
    A. so   **C.** for
    B. or   **D.** because

47. Virgil looked at the girl in the locket, _____ he asked her to save the lettuce.
    A. or   **C.** but
    B. so   **D.** and

DIRECTIONS
Find the sentence that has no mistakes. Circle the letter for the correct sentence.

48. **A.** Where Maya Lin go to school?
    B. Where do Maya Lin go to school?
    C. Where did Maya Lin go to school?
    D. Where did Maya Lin goes to school?

49. **A.** Miss Fleck was surprised, or she had never seen a garden as big as Virgil's garden.
    B. Miss Fleck was surprised, so she had never seen a garden as big as Virgil's garden.
    C. Miss Fleck was surprised, for she had never seen a garden as big as Virgil's garden.
    D. Miss Fleck was surprised, but she had never seen a garden as big as Virgil's garden.

50. **A.** Virgil wanted a new bike, so he didn't have any money.
    B. Virgil wanted a new bike, or he didn't have any money.
    C. Virgil wanted a new bike, but he didn't have any money.
    D. Virgil wanted a new bike, for he didn't have any money.

WRITING

WRITING PROMPT

Think about a time when you did something well.

Write a story to tell what happened. Tell what you did and how it felt to be successful.
Use the pronoun I in your writing. Write on the lines below.

_____

_____

_____

_____

_____

_____

_____

_____

_____

_____

_____

_____

_____

_____

_____

_____

_____

_____

_____

_____

_____

_____

STOP

UNIT 4 Test

LISTENING Passage: "A New Kind of Transportation"

DIRECTIONS

Listen to the passage. Then choose the best answer for each item. Circle the letter for the correct answer.

1. The Segway looks like a—
   - **A.** bus.
   - **B.** car.
   - **C.** scooter.
   - **D.** computer.

2. The Segway will probably be used mostly to travel—
   - **A.** into space.
   - **B.** on long trips.
   - **C.** on short trips.
   - **D.** on the highway.

3. What does the Segway use for energy?
   - **A.** gasoline
   - **B.** a battery
   - **C.** the wind
   - **D.** the sun's heat

4. What is one way that the Segway helps Earth's environment?
   - **A.** It burns fossil fuels.
   - **B.** People will always use it instead of cars.
   - **C.** It travels faster and farther than cars can travel.
   - **D.** It uses a cleaner source of energy and saves fossil fuels.

GO ON ▶

PHONICS AND SPELLING

DIRECTIONS

Choose the word with the same sound as the underlined part of the word in the box. Circle the letter for the correct answer.

5. | ab**ou**t |
   A. boats
   B. affect
   C. plants
   D. messy

6. | pr**o**bl**e**m |
   A. blue
   B. pole
   C. focus
   D. sleepy

7. | hum**a**n |
   A. huge
   B. many
   C. nation
   D. school

8. | hi**s** |
   A. us
   B. this
   C. class
   D. hands

9. | y**es** |
   A. tries
   B. glass
   C. eyes
   D. teachers

DIRECTIONS

Choose the word that is spelled correctly and completes the sentence. Circle the letter for the correct answer.

10. It is important to save Earth's _____ resources.
    A. natural
    B. nateral
    C. natrual
    D. naturel

11. Hybrid cars burn less _____ than other kinds of cars.
    A. gasuline
    B. gasoline
    C. gasaline
    D. gaseline

12. If chemicals get into the water, many _____ will die.
    A. fish
    B. fishs
    C. fisheys
    D. fishies

13. I like reading _____ about characters who are like Shirley.
    A. stores
    B. storys
    C. stories
    D. storyes

14. The _____ of the lettuce plant are good to eat.
    A. leafz
    B. leaffs
    C. leafes
    D. leaves

Unit 4 Test/ Phonics and Spelling

VOCABULARY

DIRECTIONS

Choose the best answer for each item. Circle the letter for the correct answer.

15. Something that makes part of Earth's environment dirty is called—
   A. trends.
   B. pollution.
   C. technology.
   D. resources.

16. Herbicides, pesticides, and fertilizers are all—
   A. trends.
   B. proofs.
   C. chemicals.
   D. nuclear power.

17. Who is the leader of a school?
   A. a trend
   B. a proof
   C. a resource
   D. a principal

18. What is a reputation?
   A. What others think or say about a person
   B. Something good on Earth that helps living things
   C. What scientists create to help them solve problems
   D. Something people use to show that something is true

DIRECTIONS

Choose the word that best completes each sentence. Circle the letter for the correct answer.

19. Scientists are creating new ways to power cars and other _____ to help Earth's environment.
   A. wastes
   B. pollutions
   C. reputations
   D. technologies

20. Fossil fuels are one of Earth's natural _____.
   A. resources
   B. principals
   C. reputations
   D. technologies

21. The principal wanted to see _____ of Shirley's age.
   A. honor
   B. proof
   C. trend
   D. worthy

22. It is a great _____ to be an ambassador.
   A. trend
   B. proof
   C. honor
   D. worthy

GO ON

READING: "Changing Earth"

Choose the best answer for each item. Circle the letter for the correct answer.

23. "Changing Earth" is—
- **A.** fiction.
- **B.** nonfiction.
- **C.** an interview.
- **D.** historical fiction.

24. When cars, factories, and power plants burn fossil fuels, they cause—
- **A.** gasoline.
- **B.** resources.
- **C.** solar power.
- **D.** air pollution.

25. What is one effect caused by a growing human population?
- **A.** More people need food.
- **B.** People use less fossil fuel.
- **C.** Earth has more natural resources.
- **D.** Earth has fewer problems with its environment.

26. Why are scientists using genetic engineering?
- **A.** To make all-electric cars
- **B.** To increase Earth's food supply
- **C.** To make nuclear power plants safer
- **D.** To make environmentally friendly buildings

27. The problem with traditional buildings is that—
- **A.** they waste energy.
- **B.** they don't last very long.
- **C.** they use sunlight for heating.
- **D.** they don't have air-conditioning.

28. How are nuclear power, solar power, and wind power alike?
- **A.** They create radioactive waste.
- **B.** They get energy from the sun.
- **C.** They do not cause air pollution.
- **D.** They can't always make electricity.

Unit 4 Test/Reading: "Changing Earth"

READING: "The Intersection"

DIRECTIONS

Choose the best answer for each item. Circle the letter for the correct answer.

29. What is an <u>intersection</u>?
  A. A carriage pulled by horses
  B. A place where two streets cross
  C. A street where traffic goes in one direction
  D. Something that has green, yellow, and red lights

30. Who wrote the second letter?
  A. The son of the writer of the first letter
  B. The father of the writer of the first letter
  C. The brother of the writer of the first letter
  D. The grandfather of the writer of the first letter

31. Which of these is <u>not</u> a problem with the intersection?
  A. People drive too fast.
  B. People have accidents.
  C. The intersection is noisy.
  D. There are too many traffic lights.

32. What do all three letter writers want people to do?
  A. Drive more slowly through the intersection
  B. Ask the city to buy new traffic lights for the intersection
  C. Honk their horns before driving through the intersection
  D. Not sell old houses to people who build apartment buildings

GO ON

READING: "China's Little Ambassador"

DIRECTIONS
Choose the best answer for each item. Circle the letter for the correct answer.

33. How does Shirley feel at the beginning of the passage?
- **A.** Sick
- **B.** Happy
- **C.** Angry
- **D.** Nervous

34. Read this sentence from the passage.
Suddenly, Mother hissed in Chinese, "Stop that or else!"
This sentence is an example of—
- **A.** a simile.
- **B.** dialogue.
- **C.** a flashback.
- **D.** words that rhyme.

35. Which sentence from the passage is a simile?
- **A.** Shirley bowed deeply.
- **B.** "No," she said much too quickly.
- **C.** Several others were thin as chopsticks.
- **D.** She imagined herself on a boat back to China.

36. What problem does Shirley have in class?
- **A.** She doesn't like her teacher, Mrs. Rappaport.
- **B.** She can't understand all that Mrs. Rappaport says.
- **C.** She can't see the math problems on the chalkboard.
- **D.** She doesn't know the answers to any of the math problems.

37. When Shirley opens and shuts both eyes, Mrs. Rappaport thinks that Shirley—
- **A.** is feeling sick.
- **B.** is trying to be friendly.
- **C.** has a problem seeing things.
- **D.** doesn't know how to shut only one eye.

38. When you ask yourself whether you have had the same thoughts and feelings as Shirley, you are—
- **A.** previewing and predicting.
- **B.** skimming a text to find main ideas.
- **C.** noting causes, effects, and solutions.
- **D.** using your experience to understand a story.

READING: "Migration Patterns"

DIRECTIONS
Choose the best answer for each item. Circle the letter for the correct answer.

39. "Migration Patterns" is —
- **A.** an interview.
- **B.** historical fiction.
- **C.** a letter to the editor.
- **D.** an informational text.

40. According to the passage, which statement is true?
- **A.** Young adults move more often than older adults.
- **B.** Rich people move more often than poor people.
- **C.** Married people move more often than single people.
- **D.** People usually move to another country when they move.

41. What does the author predict will happen to the Northeast in the future?
- **A.** Its population will get larger.
- **B.** Its population will get smaller.
- **C.** Its population will stay about the same.
- **D.** Many Southerners will move to the Northeast.

42. Look at the bar graph. Which group moved the least often from March 1999 to 2000?
- **A.** People who were 65 to 84 years old
- **B.** People who were 85 years old or older
- **C.** People who were 1 to 4 years old
- **D.** People who were 20 to 24 years old

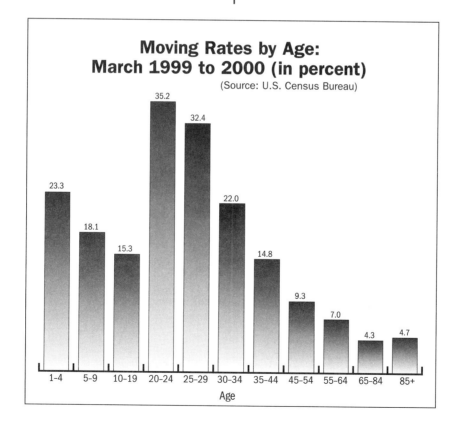

**Moving Rates by Age:
March 1999 to 2000 (in percent)**
(Source: U.S. Census Bureau)

Age	Percent
1–4	23.3
5–9	18.1
10–19	15.3
20–24	35.2
25–29	32.4
30–34	22.0
35–44	14.8
45–54	9.3
55–64	7.0
65–84	4.3
85+	4.7

GRAMMAR

DIRECTIONS

Choose the word or words that best complete each sentence. Circle the letter for the correct answer.

43. If a building uses sunlight and ventilation instead of furnaces and air-conditioning, it _____ energy.
    A. saved   **B.** save   **C.** saves   **D.** saving

44. Earth will have less fossil fuel if more cars _____ gasoline.
    A. burn   **B.** burns   **C.** burning   **D.** will burn

45. If people drive too fast, they _____ more accidents.
    A. had   **B.** having   **C.** will has   **D.** will have

DIRECTIONS

Choose the best answer for each item. Circle the letter for the correct answer.

46. Which of these is an independent clause?
    A. Shirley put up ten fingers.   **C.** Because she was a new student
    B. After Shirley's mother left   **D.** While the principal filled out a form

47. Which of these is a complex sentence?
    A. The class stood up and waved.
    B. When the principal looked at Shirley and her mother
    C. Shirley handed the note to Father, and he read it aloud.
    D. As Shirley put on her coat, Mrs. Rappaport gave her a letter.

DIRECTIONS

Find the sentence that has no mistakes. Circle the letter for the correct sentence.

48. **A.** If we use solar-powered cars, Earth's air be cleaner.
    B. If we use solar-powered cars, Earth's air being cleaner.
    C. If we use solar-powered cars, Earth's air will be cleaner.
    D. If we uses solar-powered cars, Earth's air will be cleaner.

49. **A.** Shirley wrote the correct answer, Mrs. Rappaport smiled at her.
    B. When Shirley wrote the correct answer, Mrs. Rappaport smiled at her.
    C. When, Shirley wrote the correct answer, Mrs. Rappaport smiled at her.
    D. When Shirley wrote the correct answer. Mrs. Rappaport smiled at her,

50. **A.** Shirley's hands shake she gives Father the letter.
    B. Shirley's hands shake as she gives Father the letter.
    C. Shirley's hands shake as she giving Father the letter.
    D. Shirley's hands shake as she the letter gives to Father.

WRITING

WRITING PROMPT

Think about a change that will make your school better.

Write a formal persuasive letter to your principal about changing the way something is done at school. Explain what the change is and why this change is needed. Use persuasive reasons that support your ideas. Include all the parts of a formal letter. Write on the lines below.

_____

_____

_____

_____

_____

_____

_____

_____

_____

_____

_____

_____

_____

_____

_____

_____

_____

_____

_____

STOP

UNIT 5 Test

LISTENING Passage: "Jesse's Journal"

DIRECTIONS
Listen to the passage. Then choose the best answer for each item. Circle the letter for the correct answer.

1. What is the passage mostly about?
   A. Life in Abilene, Kansas
   B. How to stop a cattle stampede
   C. Ranchers selling cattle in the east
   D. Cowboys moving cattle to Kansas

2. What caused the cattle to stampede?
   A. A thunderstorm started.
   B. The cowboys waved their hats.
   C. The cattle didn't want to get wet.
   D. The cowboys shot their guns in the air.

3. How does Jesse feel by the end of the passage?
   A. Tired
   B. Angry
   C. Scared
   D. Worried

4. You can tell from this passage that—
   A. most cowboys are wealthy.
   B. cattle are always calm and quiet.
   C. cowboys usually work long, hard days.
   D. cooks on cattle drives make good food.

GO ON

PHONICS AND SPELLING

DIRECTIONS

Choose the word with the same sound as the underlined part of the word in the box. Circle the letter for the correct answer.

5. | crop |
A. car
B. cry
C. rock
D. corn

6. | flour |
A. full
B. loaf
C. shelf
D. floor

7. | plea |
A. pole
B. leap
C. plant
D. palace

8. | watch |
A. each
B. thick
C. school
D. clothes

9. | where |
A. were
B. wish
C. what
D. write

DIRECTIONS

Choose the word that is spelled correctly and completes the sentence. Circle the letter for the correct answer.

10. Lucinda is _____ than her brother Willis.
A. friendlier
B. friendiler
C. friendyler
D. friendlyer

11. Willis is the _____ person in Lucinda's family.
A. angrest
B. angrist
C. angriest
D. angryest

12. My little brother is the _____ boy I have ever seen.
A. happist
B. happiest
C. happyist
D. happyest

13. Bill's family didn't _____ where he was.
A. kow
B. now
C. nkow
D. know

14. The cowboy cut the rope with a _____.
A. nife
B. knife
C. nkife
D. kanife

VOCABULARY

DIRECTIONS

Choose the best answer for each item. Circle the letter for the correct answer.

15. What is <u>patriotism</u>?
    - **A.** The leader of a government
    - **B.** A fight between two armies
    - **C.** Positive feelings about your country
    - **D.** The fear of being killed in battle

16. A country with a government and a president elected by the people is called a—
    - **A.** siege.
    - **B.** promise.
    - **C.** republic.
    - **D.** constitution.

17. Which word describes a feeling of love or caring for someone or something?
    - **A.** curious
    - **B.** promise
    - **C.** political
    - **D.** affection

18. When you want to find out more about something, you are feeling—
    - **A.** curious.
    - **B.** enforce.
    - **C.** political.
    - **D.** affection.

DIRECTIONS

Choose the word that best completes each sentence. Circle the letter for the correct answer.

19. The American settlers didn't obey Mexican laws, so Mexican soldiers came to Texas to _____ the laws.
    - **A.** siege
    - **B.** enforce
    - **C.** promise
    - **D.** constitution

20. The Mexican army surrounded the Alamo and began a _____ that lasted for many days.
    - **A.** siege
    - **B.** promise
    - **C.** republic
    - **D.** constitution

21. Grandy and the other coyotes sleep in a _____.
    - **A.** den
    - **B.** siege
    - **C.** promise
    - **D.** curious

22. A man who moves cattle from one place to another is called a _____.
    - **A.** pack
    - **B.** ranch
    - **C.** cowboy
    - **D.** promise

GO ON

READING: "The Road to Texas Independence"

DIRECTIONS
Choose the best answer for each item. Circle the letter for the correct answer.

23. What is "The Road to Texas Independence" mostly about?
- **A.** Texas becoming a state
- **B.** The battle at the Alamo
- **C.** The life of Sam Houston
- **D.** The land and weather in Texas

24. Which of these statements about the battle at the Alamo is <u>not</u> true?
- **A.** The battle lasted for many days.
- **B.** Everyone inside the Alamo was killed during the battle.
- **C.** William Travis refused to surrender to the Mexican army.
- **D.** The Mexican army had many more soldiers than the Texan army.

25. Texas soldiers yelled "Remember the Alamo!" during the battle at San Jacinto because they wanted to—
- **A.** help others find the Alamo fort.
- **B.** help others find the Mexican soldiers.
- **C.** show their anger about a terrible battle that Texas had lost.
- **D.** show their pride about an important battle that Texas had won.

26. Santa Anna surrendered to Sam Houston just after—
- **A.** the battle at the Alamo.
- **B.** the battle at San Jacinto.
- **C.** Texas became a state in the United States.
- **D.** the first battle between Texas and Mexico.

27. Why should you take notes about the dates and events in "The Road to Texas Independence"?
- **A.** To preview the text
- **B.** To figure out the meanings of words
- **C.** To remember the time order of events
- **D.** To help predict which event will happen next

28. You can tell "The Road to Texas Independence" is nonfiction because it—
- **A.** tells about people living in Texas.
- **B.** tells about soldiers fighting in a war.
- **C.** tells about a real place, but imaginary people.
- **D.** gives facts about real people, places, and events.

READING: from *A Line in the Sand*

DIRECTIONS
Choose the best answer for each item. Circle the letter for the correct answer.

29. Where did the events in this story take place?
    A. In San Felipe
    B. At a military fort
    C. At a town meeting
    D. On the Lawrences' farm

30. Why did Lucinda's father join the Peace Party?
    A. He likes the way Mexico rules Texas.
    B. He wants Texas to become its own nation.
    C. He doesn't want Texas to have a war with Mexico.
    D. He enjoys arguing with Uncle Henry about Texas's future.

31. When Texas goes to war with Mexico, Willis will probably—
    A. join the Peace Party.
    B. join the Texan army.
    C. join the Mexican army.
    D. move back to the United States.

32. The journal entries in *The Line in the Sand* are historical fiction because—
    A. journal entries are always historical fiction.
    B. the people, places, and events in the journal are all imaginary.
    C. the characters are not real, but the information about Texas is true.
    D. the characters are real, but the information about Texas is not true.

READING: from *Pecos Bill: The Greatest Cowboy of All Time*

DIRECTIONS
Choose the best answer for each item. Circle the letter for the correct answer.

33. What happens to Pecos Bill when he is four years old?
    A. He plans to become a great cowboy.
    B. He becomes the leader of the coyotes.
    C. He is chased by the Wouser and gets hurt.
    D. He falls out of his family's wagon and gets lost.

34. You can tell from the passage that Grandy—
    A. is not liked by the other coyotes.
    B. trusts coyotes, but not other animals.
    C. likes Pecos Bill and takes good care of him.
    D. does not like being the leader of the coyotes.

35. Which sentence is the best summary for the middle of the passage?
    A. Grandy shows Bill some sweet berries.
    B. Grandy teaches Bill about being a coyote.
    C. Grandy shows Bill where to find bird eggs.
    D. Grandy teaches Bill how to move very fast.

36. Which group of words from the passage is an example of hyperbole?
    A. Berries that were good to eat
    B. The greatest cowboy of all time
    C. An old covered wagon with wheels
    D. Westward through Texas in the early days

37. You can tell that the passage is a tall tale because—
    A. all the characters are tall.
    B. the characters are imaginary.
    C. some of the characters are animals.
    D. the characters have exaggerated qualities.

38. Why did the author write *Pecos Bill: The Greatest Cowboy of All Time*?
    A. To give facts about a real cowboy
    B. To make readers laugh at a funny story
    C. To persuade readers not to harm coyotes
    D. To describe real animals that live in Texas

READING: "The Cowboy Era"

DIRECTIONS

Choose the best answer for each item. Circle the letter for the correct answer.

39. Why were cattle worth more money in the northern and eastern United States?
  A. People in those areas did not raise many cattle.
  B. People in those areas ate more beef than people in Texas.
  C. There were only a few longhorn cattle in the United States.
  D. People in those areas were richer than people in other areas.

40. Which sentence does <u>not</u> describe a cowboy's life during the cowboy era?
  A. They worked long days.
  B. They got paid well for their work.
  C. Some cowboys died while driving cattle north.
  D. They had to fight people who tried to steal the cattle.

41. Why did cowboys on cattle drives sometimes cover their noses and mouths with bandannas?
  A. To keep out the dust in the air
  B. To make themselves look nice
  C. So they wouldn't scare the cattle
  D. So no one would know who they were

42. The great cattle drives ended because of an increase in Texas's—
  A. cowboys.
  B. cattle rustlers.
  C. cattle stampedes.
  D. fences and railroads.

GO ON ▶

GRAMMAR

DIRECTIONS
Choose the word or words that best complete each sentence. Circle the letter for the correct answer.

43. Texas is _____ Kansas.
- **A.** large than
- **B.** the largest
- **C.** larger than
- **D.** more larger

44. Stephen F. Austin is one of the _____ people in Texas history.
- **A.** famouser
- **B.** most famous
- **C.** more famouser
- **D.** most famousest

45. This year's cotton crop was the _____ crop the family had ever grown.
- **A.** best
- **B.** better
- **C.** bestest
- **D.** most best

46. These red boots are mine, and those brown boots are _____.
- **A.** her
- **B.** our
- **C.** your
- **D.** yours

47. A coyote is a wild animal, and _____ hearing is very good.
- **A.** its
- **B.** hers
- **C.** ours
- **D.** mine

DIRECTIONS
Find the sentence that has no mistakes. Circle the letter for the correct sentence.

48.
- **A.** Cowboys wear hers hats for protection in bad weather.
- **B.** Cowboys wear mine hats for protection in bad weather.
- **C.** Cowboys wear their hats for protection in bad weather.
- **D.** Cowboys wear theirs hats for protection in bad weather.

49.
- **A.** This land is his, and that ranch is my.
- **B.** This land is his, and that ranch is hers.
- **C.** This land is our, and that ranch is yours.
- **D.** This land is yours, and that ranch is their.

50.
- **A.** I think Texas wildflowers are pretty than roses.
- **B.** I think Texas wildflowers are prettier than roses.
- **C.** I think Texas wildflowers are more prettier than roses.
- **D.** I think Texas wildflowers are the most prettiest than roses.

GO ON

Unit 5 Test/Grammar

WRITING

> ### WRITING PROMPT
> Think about your life today and life in Texas in the 1800s. Do you think life today is easier than life in Texas long ago?
>
> Write one or two paragraphs about your life today. Tell whether you think life today is easier or harder than life in Texas long ago. Give reasons for your opinion. Include details in your writing. Write on the lines below.

_____

_____

_____

_____

_____

_____

_____

_____

_____

_____

_____

_____

_____

_____

_____

_____

_____

_____

STOP

UNIT 6 Test

LISTENING Passage: "The Sun and the Stars (A South African Myth)"

DIRECTIONS

Listen to the passage. Then choose the best answer for each item. Circle the letter for the correct answer.

1. You can tell that the man was powerful because he—
   A. was old.
   B. lived long ago.
   C. took long naps.
   D. made bright light.

2. Why did the people get cold?
   A. The man went to live high up in the sky.
   B. When the man slept, he blew cold winds.
   C. When the man slept, there was no warm light.
   D. The people hid underground to escape the man.

3. What happened to the man when the children threw him up into the sky?
   A. He became the sun.
   B. He grew old and tired.
   C. He stopped making light.
   D. He was badly burned by the sun.

4. What natural event does this myth explain?
   A. why the moon shines so brightly
   B. why there are seasons on Earth
   C. how Earth moves around the sun
   D. how the sun and stars got in the sky

GO ON

PHONICS AND SPELLING

DIRECTIONS

Choose the word with the same sound as the underlined part of the word in the box. Circle the letter for the correct answer.

5. | di̲sh̲ |
   A. brush
   B. hands
   C. school
   D. wheels

6. | p̲hone |
   A. shop
   B. push
   C. photo
   D. hopes

7. | th̲at |
   A. with
   B. those
   C. watch
   D. thumb

8. | d̲ow̲n |
   A. won
   B. wood
   C. know
   D. house

9. | c̲oi̲n |
   A. nice
   B. cook
   C. enjoy
   D. moving

DIRECTIONS

Choose the word that is spelled correctly and completes the sentence. Circle the letter for the correct answer.

10. The Wawaniki people grew _____ because they had no food.
   A. hin
   B. tin
   C. thin
   D. twin

11. The man climbed a _____ to fix our roof.
   A. lader
   B. ladter
   C. lather
   D. ladder

12. I bought a _____ for the school play.
   A. ticket
   B. sticket
   C. tricket
   D. thicket

13. The adventurers are _____ all the contests.
   A. wining
   B. winiing
   C. winning
   D. wininng

14. The khan is _____ with anger.
   A. shaking
   B. shakeing
   C. shakking
   D. shakkeing

GO ON

VOCABULARY

DIRECTIONS

**Choose the best answer for each question.
Circle the letter for the correct answer.**

15. What is the <u>equator</u>?
  A. The turning of Earth on its axis
  B. Something that makes Earth shake and crack
  C. An imaginary line through the North and South Poles
  D. An imaginary line halfway between the North and South Poles

16. The path Earth follows around the sun is called—
  A. an axis.
  B. an orbit.
  C. the pole.
  D. a rotation.

17. What is another word that means the same as <u>game</u>?
  A. axis
  B. orbit
  C. contest
  D. rotation

18. What do you call a person who likes to do exciting things?
  A. a realm
  B. a match
  C. a palace
  D. an adventurer

DIRECTIONS

**Choose the word or words that best
complete each sentence. Circle the letter
for the correct answer.**

19. The half of Earth that is south of the equator is the _____.
  A. summer
  B. South Pole
  C. Southern Hemisphere
  D. Northern Hemisphere

20. The turning of Earth on its axis is Earth's _____.
  A. orbit
  B. realm
  C. equator
  D. rotation

21. The khan lives in a large _____ in a beautiful city.
  A. palace
  B. contest
  C. conquer
  D. adventurer

22. The khan wants his army to _____ his enemies and take their land.
  A. fear
  B. conquer
  C. adventurer
  D. run away from

GO ON

READING: "Earth's Orbit"

DIRECTIONS
Choose the best answer for each item. Circle the letter for the correct answer.

23. Earth makes one complete rotation on its axis in one—
  A. day.
  B. hour.
  C. year.
  D. month.

24. Earth revolves around—
  A. the sun.
  B. the moon.
  C. its equator.
  D. the North Star.

25. Look at this diagram. What do the two arrows on the left show?
  A. How sunlight hits Earth
  B. Where the North Pole is
  C. Where the South Pole is
  D. How Earth rotates on its axis

26. Why is it usually hot near the equator?
  A. There is no wind at the equator.
  B. That area gets less direct sunlight.
  C. That area gets more direct sunlight.
  D. That area does not get much rain.

27. When does the Southern Hemisphere have winter?
  A. When the Northern Hemisphere has winter
  B. When that hemisphere gets more direct sunlight
  C. When that hemisphere is tilted away from the sun
  D. When that hemisphere is tilted toward the sun

28. During an equinox, the sun is directly above—
  A. the equator.
  B. Earth's axis.
  C. the South Pole.
  D. the North Pole.

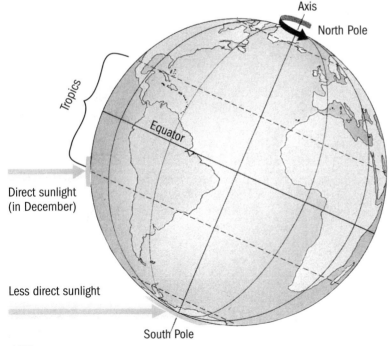

Axis
North Pole
Tropics
Equator
Direct sunlight (in December)
Less direct sunlight
South Pole

As Earth orbits the sun, sunlight always hits the area around the equator (the tropics) more directly than it hits areas farther from the equator.

GO ON

READING: "How Glooskap Found the Summer" and "Persephone and the Pomegranate Seeds"

DIRECTIONS

Choose the best answer for each item. Circle the letter for the correct answer.

"How Glooskap Found the Summer"

29. Why does Glooskap go to Winter's wigwam at the beginning of the story?
    A. To get Winter to help him sleep better
    B. To get Winter to fight against Summer
    C. To get Winter to make the land less cold
    D. To listen to Winter's stories about old times

30. Why is Glooskap a hero?
    A. He talks to Tatler the Loon.
    B. He finds Winter in a land far north.
    C. He falls asleep in Winter's wigwam.
    D. He gets Summer to make Winter go away.

"Persephone and the Pomegranate Seeds"

31. The conflict in this passage is about—
    A. where Pluto will live.
    B. where Persephone will live.
    C. Demeter getting married to Zeus.
    D. Zeus sending Hermes to the underworld.

32. "How Glooskap Found the Summer" and "Persephone and the Pomegranate Seeds" are both—
    A. myths.
    B. mysteries.
    C. biographies.
    D. science articles.

READING: *The Great Bear*

DIRECTIONS
Choose the best answer for each item. Circle the letter for the correct answer.

33. What does the narrator do in *The Great Bear*?
 A. Tests the skills of the Adventurers
 B. Explains where characters go and who they meet
 C. Shoots a bird out of the sky using a bow and arrow
 D. Tells how actors should say their lines and move onstage

34. What happens in the first scene in *The Great Bear*?
 A. The adventurers meet one another.
 B. The khan decides to test the adventurers.
 C. The khan tries to kill the adventurers in a fire.
 D. The adventurers become stars in a constellation.

35. How does Great Listener help the other adventurers?
 A. She wins a contest with her great hearing.
 B. She puts out the fire and saves the other adventurers.
 C. She hears Khan's plans and tells others about them.
 D. She listens to the adventurers and explains their ideas to others.

36. Which of the following is an example of a stage direction?
 A. **SCENE 2**
 B. **KHAN'S SON:**
 C. *(KHAN and KHAN'S SON pantomime talking together.)*
 D. Father, today I met several young adventurers who want to serve you.

37. Why is this play called *The Great Bear*?
 A. The khan looks like a big, mean bear.
 B. The adventurers become stars in a constellation with the shape of a bear.
 C. Mountain Lifter has to wrestle a big, strong bear in one of the khan's contests.
 D. The khan puts a great bear in the banquet room to try to kill the adventurers.

38. Before you begin reading a play aloud, you use the list of characters to figure out—
 A. how actors should move onstage.
 B. how actors should read their lines.
 C. when actors should say their lines.
 D. how many actors you need for the play.

READING: "Telescopes"

DIRECTIONS
Choose the best answer for each item. Circle the letter for the correct answer.

39. What does a refracting telescope use to collect light?
- **A.** A mirror
- **B.** A flashlight
- **C.** A convex lens
- **D.** An eyepiece lens

40. In a reflecting telescope, light rays bounce off—
- **A.** a glass.
- **B.** a mirror.
- **C.** a convex lens.
- **D.** an eyepiece lens.

41. Why should you cover a flashlight with red cellophane when looking at stars?
- **A.** It makes things that are far away look bigger.
- **B.** It makes the light from the flashlight much brighter.
- **C.** It lets you look at the stars without damaging your eyes.
- **D.** It helps you see in the dark without affecting your night vision.

42. "Telescopes" is—
- **A.** nonfiction.
- **B.** science fiction.
- **C.** historical fiction.
- **D.** an autobiography.

GO ON

GRAMMAR

DIRECTIONS
Find the sentence that has no mistakes. Circle the letter for the correct sentence.

43. **A.** "Do you know where Summer lives? asked Glooskap.
     B. "Do you know where Summer lives? asked Glooskap."
     C. Do you know where Summer lives? "asked Glooskap."
     D. "Do you know where Summer lives?" asked Glooskap.

44. **A.** I'll make them fall asleep, Winter thought.
     B. "I'll make them fall asleep," Winter thought.
     C. "I'll make them fall asleep, Winter thought."
     D. "I'll make them fall asleep," Winter thought."

45. **A.** Winter cried, "My power is gone!"
     B. "Winter cried, My power is gone!"
     C. "Winter cried," My power is gone!
     D. "Winter cried," "My power is gone!"

46. **A.** "I ate only six seeds, Persephone replied.
     B. "I ate only six seeds, Persephone" replied.
     C. "I ate only six seeds, Persephone replied."
     D. "I ate only six seeds," Persephone replied.

DIRECTIONS
Choose the word that best completes each sentence. Circle the letter for the correct answer.

47. The adventurers became stars _____ the sky.
     A. at   **C.** with
     B. in   **D.** about

48. Mountain Lifter is a man _____ strong arms.
     A. at   **C.** with
     B. in   **D.** about

49. We watched the stars _____ night.
     A. at   **C.** on
     B. in   **D.** under

50. The sky is full _____ stars tonight.
     A. at   **C.** on
     B. in   **D.** of

WRITING

WRITING PROMPT

Think of some characters with special skills. Then think of a problem these characters could solve.

Write a story about two or more characters who use their special skills to solve a problem. Tell what the problem is and how the characters solve the problem. Include dialogue in your writing. Write on the lines below.

_____

_____

_____

_____

_____

_____

_____

_____

_____

_____

_____

_____

_____

_____

_____

_____

_____

_____

_____

_____

_____

_____

STOP

Shining Star ★ B

Test Preparation

Test Preparation

TAKING A TEST

Strategy: Understand Directions Before You Take a Test

Most tests have directions that tell you what to do. Sometimes your teacher will read the directions to you. Other times you will read them yourself. Listen or read carefully. Be sure you understand the directions before you begin the test.

> Understanding directions before you take the test will help you
> * know what to do on a test.
> * answer questions correctly.

Practice this strategy by answering the questions on the next page. Follow these steps:

1. Listen to or read the directions carefully.
2. Look for important words in the directions.
3. If you don't understand a word, use context clues to help you figure out the meaning of the word. Context clues are the words that come before and after the word you don't know.
4. Raise your hand and ask for help if you don't understand the directions.
5. Follow the directions to answer each question.
6. Sometimes directions change. Look for new directions as you read. Repeat steps 1–5 above each time you see new directions.
7. Look for directions at the bottom of the page.

   If you see **GO ON**, it means you should go on to answer the questions on the next page.

   If you see **STOP**, do not go on to the next page. If you finish a test early, you can go back and check your answers.

Name _____ Date _____

DIRECTIONS
Read the words inside and outside each oval. Find the missing word. Circle the letter for the correct answer.

1. Find the missing word.

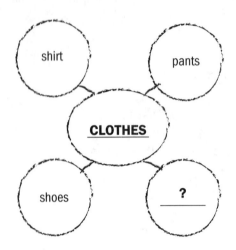

A. coat
B. book
C. game
D. ring

2. Find the missing word.

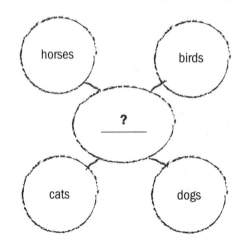

A. animals
B. people
C. places
D. fish

DIRECTIONS
Choose the word with the same sound as the underlined part of the word in the box. Circle the letter for the correct answer.

3. w<u>i</u>fe
  A. this
  B. winter
  C. five
  D. river

4. pl<u>ay</u>
  A. land
  B. farm
  C. head
  D. make

DIRECTIONS
Read the pair of sentences. Look at the underlined word in the first sentence. Then choose the correct pronoun to complete the second sentence. Circle the letter for the correct answer.

5. <u>Kenny</u> takes care of his little sister after school. _____ plays games with her.
  A. He **B.** She **C.** Him **D.** Her

DIRECTIONS
Find the sentence that does not have any mistakes. Circle the letter for the correct answer.

6. A. Austin or Houston are two cities in Texas.
   B. Austin not Houston are two cities in Texas.
   C. Austin but Houston are two cities in Texas.
   D. Austin and Houston are two cities in Texas.

Test Preparation/Strategy: Understand Directions Before You Take a Test

Test Preparation

ANSWERING QUESTIONS ABOUT A PASSAGE

Strategy: Preview the Title, Passage, and Questions

Some tests have passages, or readings, such as short stories, poems, or history or science texts. The tests also have questions or items that ask about the passages. Before you read each passage, preview the title, the passage, and the questions. When you preview, you look at the title, the passage, and the questions to find out what the passage is about and what the questions ask.

Previewing the title, the passage, and the questions will help you
- decide how to read the passage.
- think about what you will need to know to answer the questions.

Practice this strategy by answering the questions on the next page. Follow these steps:

1. Look at the title and the first sentence in each paragraph in the passage. Ask yourself, "Is this passage fiction or nonfiction? What is this passage mostly about?"

2. Then decide how to read the passage. If the passage is nonfiction, or if it tells about something you don't know much about, you should read the passage slowly and carefully. If the passage is fiction, or if it tells about something you already know, you can probably read the passage more quickly.

3. Look at any art that goes with the passage, such as a picture, a chart, or a map. Ask yourself, "What does the art tell me about the passage?"

4. Look at the questions. Find out what information you need to know to answer the questions. For example, find out if you need to know about the main idea or a character's feelings. Then look for this information as you read the passage.

5. Read the passage. Don't worry if you do not understand all the words. You need to understand enough information to answer the questions.

6. Follow the directions to answer each question. Look back at the passage as often as you like to help you answer the questions. You don't have to reread the whole passage. Look for information that helps you answer the questions. If you are allowed to write in your test, underline key words that help you answer the questions.

7. Don't spend too much time on a question. If you can't decide what the best answer is, circle the number of the question. If you have time at the end of the test, you can go back and finish any questions you circled.

DIRECTIONS
Read the passage. Then choose the best answer for each item. Circle the letter for the correct answer.

Frieda's Special Birthday Present

Frieda told her parents that she wanted a puppy for her birthday. Her parents weren't sure if they should give Frieda a puppy. They didn't know if Frieda could take care of a young pet. Dad told Frieda, "A puppy is a lot of work. You have to walk it and feed it every day."

Frieda said, "I can take good care of a puppy. I know I can do a good job!"

On her birthday, Frieda got some nice presents, but she didn't get a puppy. Then Mom said, "Wait a minute. Your father has one more present for you." Frieda heard barking! Dad came into the room and put a small, brown puppy on the floor.

"Happy Birthday!" her parents said. Frieda smiled as the puppy licked her hand. She loved the puppy, and she was glad that her parents believed she could take care of it.

1. This passage is—
   A. a play.
   B. fiction.
   C. a poem.
   D. a history text.

2. You can tell from the title that this passage is about—
   A. taking care of a puppy.
   B. making a birthday present.
   C. the day Frieda was born.
   D. a birthday present for Frieda.

3. Frieda's parents weren't sure they should give Frieda a puppy because—
   A. they did not want to have a pet.
   B. Frieda does not like dogs.
   C. they thought the puppy would make a big mess.
   D. they did not know if Frieda could take care of a puppy.

4. How does Frieda feel at the end?
   A. Nervous
   B. Happy
   C. Upset
   D. Tired

Test Preparation

ANSWERING MULTIPLE-CHOICE QUESTIONS

Strategy: Read, Think, Look, and Choose

A multiple-choice question has three or four answer choices, but only one choice is the correct answer. You have to choose the best answer for each question. To answer a multiple-choice question, remember to *read* the question, *think* about the correct answer, *look* at all the answer choices, and then *choose* the best answer.

> Reading, thinking, looking, and choosing will help you
> * use your own knowledge to answer the question.
> * choose the best answer for the question.

Practice this strategy by answering the questions on the next page. Follow these steps:

1. Read the question.
2. Cover up the answer choices with your hand.
3. Think of the correct answer.
4. After you have an idea of the correct answer, move your hand and look at the answer choices. Read each choice. Find the answer choice that is closest to your answer. This choice should be the best answer.
5. If the question asks about a passage and you are not sure of the answer, look back at the passage to try to find information that answers the question.
6. Don't spend too much time on a question. If you can't decide what the best answer is, circle the number of the question. You can come back to answer this question later, if you have time.
7. When you finish answering all the questions, check your answers. If you have carefully thought about all the answer choices for a question, then the first answer you chose is the one most likely to be correct.

Name _____ Date _____

DIRECTIONS
Read the passage. Then choose the best answer for each item. Circle the letter for the correct answer.

How Armadillo Got His Shell

Long ago, Armadillo was a furry animal. One day, he chased Spider. Spider crawled under a bush with sharp thorns. Spider knew that Armadillo would not go under the bush because the sharp thorns would scratch Armadillo's furry skin. Armadillo waited for Spider to come out. He began to get hungry. Armadillo stretched his tongue as far as it would go, but it was not long enough to reach Spider.

Then Turtle passed under the bush.

"Don't the thorns scratch you?" Armadillo asked.

"Oh, no," Turtle replied. "My shell is very thick. The thorns can't scratch me."

"Where can *I* find a thick shell like yours?" Armadillo asked.

Turtle told Armadillo, "Wait for some rain and roll in the mud. Then lie in the hot sun. The sun will turn the mud into a thick shell."

So Armadillo followed Turtle's directions. To this day, all armadillos have thick shells to protect them wherever they go.

1. What problem does Armadillo have in this passage?
   A. He is afraid of Spider.
   B. He is tired from chasing Spider.
   C. He can't reach Spider under the thorn bush.
   D. Turtle will not let Armadillo get near Spider.

2. Spider crawled under the bush with thorns because—
   A. it was cool under the bush.
   B. he thought Armadillo would stay away.
   C. he wanted to be near his friend Turtle.
   D. he thought Armadillo couldn't see him.

3. Turtle doesn't get scratched by the thorns because—
   A. he moves slowly.
   B. he is not very big.
   C. his thick shell protects him.
   D. he digs under the bush.

4. How does Armadillo change by the end of the story?
   A. He doesn't chase Spider anymore.
   B. He stays away from bushes with thorns.
   C. He and Turtle become best friends.
   D. He gets a hard shell that protects him.

Test Preparation/Strategy: Read, Think, Look, and Choose

Test Preparation

ANSWERING QUESTIONS ABOUT MEANINGS OF WORDS

Strategy: Use Context Clues

Some tests have questions that ask about the meanings of words. Use context clues to help you figure out the meaning of a word that is unfamiliar to you. Context clues are the words before and after the word you don't know. They help explain the meaning of the word.

Using context clues will help you
- figure out the meaning of a word you don't know.
- choose the best answer for a question about the meaning of a word.

Practice this strategy by answering the questions on the next page. Follow these steps:

1. Read the question. Find the word the question asks about. This word is sometimes a word that you don't know.
2. Skim the passage quickly to find the word the question asks about.
3. Look at the words before and after the word that you don't know. Look for clues that help explain the meaning of the word.
4. Read the answer choices. Find the answer choice that gives the best meaning of the word.
5. Some questions ask you to find another word that means the *same* as the word in the question. For these questions, follow steps 1–3 above. Then compare the word in the question to the words in the answer choices. Find the word in the answer choices that has a meaning that is the same or almost the same as the word in the question. For example, *big* and *large* have the same meanings.
6. Some questions ask you to find the word that means the *opposite* of the word in the question. For these questions, follow steps 1–3 above. Then think about the meaning of each of the answer choices. The answer choice that has the meaning that is the most different from the meaning of the word in the question is the best answer. For example, *unhappy* is the opposite of *happy*, and *up* is the opposite of *down*.

Name _____ Date _____

DIRECTIONS
Read the passage. Then choose the best answer for each item. Circle the letter for the correct answer.

The Water Cycle

Most of Earth is covered with water. The amount of water on Earth never changes, but the water often changes from one form to another. For example, the water in the ocean is one <u>form</u>, or kind, of water.

The water cycle is the way that Earth's water changes its form and moves. A <u>cycle</u> is a series of things that happens over and over again in the same order. Earth's water moves from the oceans up into the air. Then it moves from the air down to the land and back into the oceans.

The sun's heat makes some of Earth's water <u>evaporate</u>. The water turns to water vapor, a gas that you can't see. The water vapor <u>rises</u> in the air. When the water vapor cools, it becomes rain, snow, sleet, or hail and falls to the land. The rain runs into lakes, rivers, and oceans. The sun's heat melts some snow and ice back to water. This water also runs into lakes, rivers, and oceans. Then the water cycle starts all over again.

In the water cycle, water changes form and moves from the oceans, lakes, and rivers up into the air. Then it changes form again and moves down to the land and back into the oceans.

1. What does the word <u>cycle</u> mean in this passage?
   A. Something that happens once
   B. Something that turns into a gas
   C. Something that you do on a bicycle
   D. Something that repeats again and again

2. When water <u>evaporates</u>, it becomes—
   A. rain.
   B. snow.
   C. a gas.
   D. a river.

3. In this passage, the word <u>form</u> means the same as—
   A. ice.
   B. many.
   C. kind.
   D. amount.

4. Which word is the opposite of the word <u>rises</u>?
   A. Falls
   B. Lifts
   C. Floats
   D. Light

Test Preparation/Strategy: Use Context Clues

Test Preparation

ANSWERING FILL-IN-THE-BLANK ITEMS

Strategy: Try Every Answer Choice

Some tests have items that give you a sentence with a word missing. You have to find the word that best completes the sentence. For these items, try every answer choice to find the word that fits best in the sentence.

> Trying every answer choice will help you
> * think about the answer choices.
> * choose the best answer for a fill-in-the-blank item.

Practice this strategy by answering the items on the next page. Follow these steps:

1. Read the item or the sentence with a missing word.
2. Look at the first answer choice. Fill in the blank in the sentence with this word. Reread the sentence with the first answer choice in the blank.
3. Ask yourself, "Does the sentence make sense with this answer choice? Does this answer choice complete the sentence correctly?"
4. Repeat steps 2 and 3 for each of the other answer choices. Find the word that best completes the sentence with a blank in it.
5. If you can write in your test, you may want to write the answer choices above the blank in the sentence so you can read the complete sentence.
6. Don't spend too much time on an item. If you can't decide what the best answer is, circle the number of the item. If you have time at the end of the test, you can go back and finish any items you circled.

GO ON ▶

Name _____ Date _____

DIRECTIONS
Read each pair of sentences. Look at the underlined word or words in the first sentence. Then choose the correct pronoun to complete the second sentence. Circle the letter for the correct answer.

1. Han and Ed play soccer. _____ are the best players on the team.
   - **A.** They
   - **B.** Him
   - **C.** He
   - **D.** It

2. The girl feeds her two <u>dogs</u>. She gives _____ food in the morning and at night.
   - **A.** her
   - **B.** it
   - **C.** them
   - **D.** us

DIRECTIONS
Choose the word that best completes each sentence. Circle the letter for the correct answer.

3. Sam _____ Lila ride to the park together.
   - **A.** or
   - **B.** and
   - **C.** but
   - **D.** with

4. During quiet time, students can either read books _____ draw pictures.
   - **A.** or
   - **B.** and
   - **C.** but
   - **D.** with

5. The _____ sun melted the ice.
   - **A.** hot
   - **B.** are
   - **C.** and
   - **D.** snow

6. Now we _____ in a blue house.
   - **A.** live
   - **B.** lives
   - **C.** lived
   - **D.** living

STOP

Test Preparation/Strategy: Try Every Answer Choice

Test Preparation

RESPONDING TO A WRITING PROMPT

Strategy: Think, Plan, Write, and Check

Some tests ask you to write about a topic. A writing test has a writing prompt with directions that tell you what to write about. When you take a writing test, *think* about the topic, *plan* what you will write about, *write* your response, and then *check* your writing.

> Thinking, planning, writing, and checking will help you
> - use your time well during a writing test.
> - write a good response.

Practice this strategy by looking at the directions on the next page and writing a response. Follow these steps:

1. Read the directions in the writing prompt. The directions tell what you should write about. Be sure you understand the directions.
2. Think about the topic. The topic is the subject or idea that the directions ask you to write about. Sometimes you can use your own experiences to help you decide what you will write.
3. Plan your writing. Sometimes your teacher will give you extra paper for planning. At other times there will be space in the test for planning. Write notes to plan what you will write about. Use a word web, a list, a chart, or an outline to help you organize your ideas.
4. Write about the topic. Be sure you do everything that the directions ask you to do.
5. When you write a short story, it should have a beginning, middle, and end. Nonfiction writing should have a main idea and supporting details. When you describe something, use adjectives that are clear and interesting. When you explain how to do something, list steps in the right order. When you try to persuade readers to do something or ask them to agree with your opinion, give good reasons that explain your ideas.
6. When you finish writing, check your work. Be sure all your sentences are complete and all words are spelled correctly.
7. Don't spend too much time on any step when writing. Find out how much time you have for the writing test. Spend some time thinking about the topic. Spend most of your time planning and writing. Be sure to leave enough time to check your writing.

WRITING PROMPT

Think of an interesting gift that someone gave to you or that you gave to someone.

Write a descriptive paragraph about this gift. Tell what the gift is and why you think it is interesting. Be sure to include details in your writing. Write on the lines below.

_____

_____

_____

_____

_____

_____

_____

_____

_____

_____

_____

_____

_____

_____

_____

_____

_____

_____

_____

_____

_____

_____

Test Preparation/Strategy: Think, Plan, Write, and Check